EXPLORE THE WONDERS OF THE MALDIVES

James Stanley

Copyright © 2024 by *James Stanley*

All rights reserved. No part of this publication may be reproduced, stored or transmitted in any form or by any means, electronic, mechanical, photocopying, recording, scanning, or otherwise without written permission from the publisher. It is illegal to copy this book, post it to a website, or distribute it by any other means without permission.

First edition 2024

CONTENTS

Introduction 5
Overview Of The Maldives .. 5
Brief History And Culture 7
Geography And Climate 10

Planning Your Trip 12
Best Time To Visit 12
Entry Requirements And Visas 14
Accommodation Options (Resorts, Guesthouses, Etc.) 17
Transportation Within The Maldives 20

Local Insights 23
Traditional Maldivian Cuisine And Dining Experiences 23
Cultural Etiquette And Customs 26
Insider Tips For Experiencing Local Life 29
Recommended Off-The-Beaten-Path Destinations . 32

Exploring The Islands 36
Popular Tourist Islands And Attractions 36
Water Activities (Snorkeling, Diving, Surfing, Etc.) 39
Land Activities (Sightseeing, Hiking, Etc.) 42
Wildlife Encounters (Marine Life, Bird Watching, Etc.) ... 45

Crafting Your Perfect Maldives Itinerary 48
Unwind In Island Bliss 49
Dive Into Underwater Wonderland 50
Family-Friendly Fun In The Sun 52
Adventure Seeker's Expedition 54

Photography Tips 56
Capturing The Beauty Of The Maldives 56
Best Times Of Day For Photography 60

- Recommended Camera Equipment 63
- Editing And Post-Processing Tips 66

Local Phrases And Language Guide 70

- Basic Greetings And Expressions 70
- Useful Phrases For Ordering Food And Shopping 73
- Cultural Nuances In Language And Communication 76
- Pronunciation Guide For Common Maldivian Words And Phrases 80

Practical Information 83

- Health And Safety Tips 83
- Currency And Money Matters 86
- Communication And Internet Access 90
- Packing Essentials And What To Bring 93

Sustainable Travel In The Maldives. 97

- Environmental Conservation Efforts 97
- Responsible Tourism Practices 101
- How Travelers Can Support Local Communities 105

Conclusion 109

- Final Thoughts And Recommendations 109
- Inspiring Travelers To Visit The Maldives 111

Travel Journal.. 116

INTRODUCTION
Overview of the Maldives

Welcome to the enchanting paradise of the Maldives, where crystal-clear turquoise waters stretch as far as the eye can see, and pristine white-sand beaches beckon travelers from across the globe. Situated in the heart of the Indian Ocean, this collection of over 1,000 coral islands is renowned for its unrivaled beauty and serenity.

Imagine a landscape straight out of a postcard: picture-perfect palm-fringed islands dotted across the azure waters, each one boasting its own unique charm and allure. Whether you're seeking a romantic getaway, a thrilling adventure, or simply a tranquil retreat, the Maldives offers an unparalleled escape from the hustle and bustle of everyday life.

But the Maldives is more than just a tropical paradise; it's a destination steeped in history, culture, and tradition. From the ancient Maldivian kingdoms to the influences of Arab, African, and South Asian traders, this archipelago has a rich and diverse heritage waiting to be discovered.

As you explore the Maldives, you'll be captivated by its vibrant underwater world. With some of the best diving and snorkeling spots in the world, the Maldives is home to an astonishing array of marine life, including colorful coral reefs, majestic manta rays, and graceful whale sharks.

Beyond its natural beauty, the Maldives is also renowned for its luxurious resorts, where you can indulge in world-class amenities, gourmet dining, and rejuvenating spa treatments. Whether you're staying in an overwater villa suspended above the lagoon or a secluded beachfront bungalow, you'll find yourself surrounded by unparalleled luxury and comfort.

But perhaps the most enchanting aspect of the Maldives is its warm and welcoming people. Known for their hospitality and generosity, the Maldivians will make you feel right at home from the moment you arrive. Immerse yourself in the local culture, savoring traditional Maldivian cuisine, learning about age-old customs and traditions, and connecting with the vibrant communities that call these islands home.

So, whether you're lounging on a sun-drenched beach, exploring the vibrant coral reefs, or simply soaking in the breathtaking beauty of the Maldivian sunset, you'll soon discover why this secluded paradise is truly a destination like no other. Welcome to the

Maldives, where every moment is an unforgettable adventure waiting to be experienced.

Brief history and culture

Embark on a journey through time and culture as we unravel the fascinating tapestry of the Maldives, a nation with a heritage as rich and diverse as its breathtaking landscapes.

The history of the Maldives is a tale of resilience, ingenuity, and adaptation, shaped by centuries of trade, exploration, and cultural exchange. Dating back over 2,000 years, the Maldives boasts a vibrant history that has left its mark on the archipelago's traditions, customs, and way of life.

Ancient seafarers from India, Arabia, and

beyond were among the first to discover the Maldives, drawn by its strategic location along key maritime trade routes. Over the centuries, these early settlers established thriving communities, cultivating a unique blend of indigenous and foreign influences that continue to define Maldivian culture to this day.

One of the most enduring legacies of the Maldives' history is its conversion to Islam in the 12th century, a pivotal moment that transformed the spiritual and cultural landscape of the archipelago. Today, Islam plays a central role in Maldivian society, shaping everything from daily rituals to social norms and governance.

But the Maldives is not just a land of ancient history; it is also a vibrant melting pot of cultures and traditions. From the colorful festivals and lively music and dance to the intricate handicrafts and exquisite cuisine, the Maldives offers a kaleidoscope of experiences that celebrate its rich cultural heritage.

Step into the bustling markets of Male, the capital city, where the sights, sounds, and smells of traditional Maldivian life come alive. Sample mouthwatering delicacies like mas huni (a savory mixture of tuna, coconut, and spices) or bondibai (sweetened rice pudding) as you immerse yourself in the flavors of the archipelago.

But perhaps the most remarkable aspect of Maldivian culture is the warmth and hospitality of its people. Known for their friendliness and generosity, the Maldivians welcome visitors with open arms, eager to share their traditions, stories, and way of life.

So whether you're exploring ancient ruins, participating in a traditional bodu beru drumming session, or simply relaxing on a secluded island paradise, you'll find yourself immersed in the vibrant tapestry of Maldivian history and culture, where every moment is a testament to the enduring spirit of this enchanting archipelago.

Geography and climate

Prepare to be enchanted by the mesmerizing geography and inviting climate of the Maldives, a paradise nestled in the heart of the Indian Ocean. From its picture-perfect islands to its tropical weather, the Maldives offers a setting that is both breathtakingly beautiful and blissfully serene.

The Maldives is an archipelago comprised of over 1,000 coral islands, grouped into 26 atolls, each one a pristine gem in its own right. As you soar above the azure waters in a seaplane or cruise along the tranquil sea aboard a dhoni, you'll be treated to a panorama of lush greenery, powdery white-sand beaches, and vibrant coral reefs stretching as far as the eye can see.

But beneath the surface lies a hidden world of unparalleled beauty and biodiversity. The Maldives is home to some of the most spectacular coral reefs on the planet, teeming with a kaleidoscope of marine life, including colorful fish, graceful sea turtles, and majestic manta rays. Whether you're snorkeling in the shallow lagoons or diving into the depths of the ocean, you'll be captivated by the sheer abundance and diversity of underwater wonders that call the Maldives home.

As for the climate, the Maldives enjoys a tropical monsoon

climate characterized by two distinct seasons: the dry season (northeast monsoon) and the wet season (southwest monsoon). The dry season, which runs from December to April, brings clear skies, gentle breezes, and balmy temperatures, making it the perfect time to visit for sun-seekers and beach lovers alike.

During the wet season, which spans from May to November, the Maldives experiences occasional rainfall and higher humidity levels, though the weather remains warm and inviting. This is also the season when the islands are blessed with lush greenery and vibrant flora, creating a verdant backdrop for outdoor adventures and eco-tourism activities.

But no matter what time of year you visit, you'll find the Maldives to be a haven of tranquility and natural beauty, where the rhythm of the ocean and the warmth of the sun are your constant companions. So pack your bags, leave your worries behind, and prepare to embark on the adventure of a lifetime in the captivating paradise of the Maldives.

PLANNING YOUR TRIP
Best time to visit

Welcome to the Maldives, where every moment is an invitation to bask in the beauty of paradise. But before you embark on your journey to this tropical haven, let's unlock the secrets of the best time to visit, ensuring you experience the Maldives at its most enchanting.

1. December to April: The Dry Season Delight

Picture-perfect weather: During the dry season, the Maldives experiences clear skies, abundant sunshine, and gentle breezes, creating the ideal conditions for sunbathing, swimming, and outdoor adventures.

Excellent visibility: The calm seas and minimal rainfall provide excellent visibility for diving and snorkeling, allowing you to explore vibrant coral reefs teeming with marine life, including colorful fish, sea turtles, and majestic manta rays.

Romantic sunsets: Toast to another day in paradise as you watch the sun dip below the horizon in a blaze of oranges, pinks, and purples, casting a magical glow over the tranquil waters of the Indian Ocean.

2. May to November: Embracing the Wet Season Wonders

Lush greenery: As the wet season sets in, the Maldives transforms into a verdant oasis, with lush greenery blanketing the islands and vibrant flora bursting into bloom, creating a picturesque backdrop for outdoor adventures and eco-tourism activities.

Fantastic diving conditions: Despite occasional rainfall, the wet season brings nutrient-rich waters and optimal diving conditions, attracting marine enthusiasts from around the world to witness spectacular underwater vistas and encounters with whale sharks and other majestic creatures.

Serene solitude: With fewer tourists visiting during the wet season, you'll have the opportunity to enjoy secluded beaches, tranquil lagoons, and uninterrupted moments of serenity, making it the perfect time for a romantic getaway or solo retreat.

Choosing the Perfect Time for Your Maldives Adventure

Personal preferences: Consider your preferred activities and experiences when choosing the best time to visit. If you're a sun-seeker who loves water sports and beach relaxation, the dry season may be ideal for you. Alternatively, if you're a nature lover who enjoys lush landscapes and diving adventures, the wet season may offer a more rewarding experience.

Budget considerations: Keep in mind that peak tourist season in the Maldives coincides with the dry season, resulting in higher prices for accommodation and activities. Traveling during the wet season may offer more affordable options and special promotions, allowing you to stretch your budget further and enjoy additional perks.

No matter when you choose to visit, the Maldives promises a journey of discovery, relaxation, and unforgettable moments, where every day is an opportunity to create cherished memories and experience the magic of paradise. So pack your bags, set your sights on adventure, and get ready to embark on the trip of a lifetime in the breathtaking Maldives!

Entry requirements and visas

Prepare to embark on an unforgettable journey to the Maldives, where azure waters, palm-fringed beaches, and endless adventures await. But before you set sail for this tropical paradise, it's essential to understand the entry requirements and visa regulations that will unlock the gateway to your dream vacation.

1. Passport Validity:

Ensure your passport is valid for at least six months beyond your intended stay in the Maldives. Passport expiration dates are strictly enforced, so double-check your documents well in advance to avoid any last-minute complications.

2. Visa Regulations:

Tourist Visa on Arrival: For most visitors, obtaining a tourist visa upon arrival in the Maldives is a hassle-free process. Upon landing at Velana International Airport in Male, you'll receive a 30-day tourist visa free of charge, allowing you to explore the wonders of the Maldives at your leisure.
Extension Options: If you wish to extend your stay beyond 30 days, you can apply for a visa extension through the Maldives Immigration Office. Extensions are typically granted for an additional 30 days, subject to approval.

3. Visa Exemptions:

Nationals of certain countries may be exempt from visa requirements for short stays in the Maldives. It's advisable to check the official website of the Maldives Immigration Service or consult with your local embassy or consulate to confirm visa exemptions based on your nationality.

4. Documentation Requirements:

In addition to a valid passport, travelers may be required to provide proof of onward travel, such as a return flight ticket, as well as evidence of sufficient funds to cover their stay in the Maldives.
Health Declarations: Due to ongoing public health concerns, travelers may be required to complete

health declarations or undergo health screenings upon arrival in the Maldives. Be prepared to comply with any additional requirements or protocols implemented by local authorities.

5. Travel Insurance:

While not a mandatory requirement for entry into the Maldives, travel insurance is highly recommended to protect yourself against unforeseen circumstances, such as medical emergencies, trip cancellations, or lost luggage. Ensure your policy provides adequate coverage for activities such as diving and water sports, which are popular pursuits in the Maldives.

6. Plan Ahead for Smooth Entry:

Familiarize yourself with entry requirements and visa regulations well in advance of your trip to the Maldives. This will help you avoid any potential delays or complications upon arrival and ensure a smooth and hassle-free entry into the country.

Keep all necessary documents, including your passport, visa, and travel insurance information, organized and easily accessible throughout your journey.

By understanding and adhering to the entry requirements and visa regulations for the Maldives, you'll lay the groundwork for a seamless and stress-free start to your tropical adventure. So pack your bags, prepare for paradise, and get ready to unlock the gateway to the breathtaking beauty of the Maldives!

Accommodation options (resorts, guesthouses, etc.)

Prepare to embark on a journey of indulgence and discovery as we explore the diverse accommodation options that await you in the Maldives. From luxurious resorts perched atop pristine atolls to charming guesthouses nestled on local islands, there's something to suit every traveler's taste and budget in this tropical paradise.

1. Luxurious Resorts:

Overwater Villas: Step into a world of opulence and elegance with a stay in one of the Maldives' iconic overwater villas. Suspended above crystal-clear lagoons, these luxurious abodes offer unrivaled privacy, breathtaking ocean views, and direct access to the vibrant underwater world below.

Private Islands: Indulge in the ultimate luxury with a stay on a private island resort, where you'll enjoy exclusive access to pristine beaches, personalized service, and an array of world-class amenities, including gourmet dining, spa treatments, and water sports facilities.

2. Secluded Retreats:

Beachfront Bungalows: Immerse yourself in the natural beauty of the Maldives with a stay in a beachfront bungalow, where you'll wake up to the sound of gentle waves lapping against the shore and panoramic views of turquoise waters stretching to the horizon.

Eco-friendly Resorts: For travelers seeking a more sustainable and eco-conscious experience, eco-friendly resorts in the Maldives offer a harmonious blend of luxury and environmental responsibility. From solar-powered villas to organic farm-to-table dining, these resorts prioritize conservation and community engagement while providing guests with a memorable and meaningful stay.

3. Authentic Experiences:

Local Guesthouses: Experience the warmth and hospitality of Maldivian culture with a stay in a local guesthouse on one of the inhabited islands. Run by friendly and welcoming hosts, these guesthouses offer an authentic glimpse into everyday life in the Maldives, with comfortable accommodations, home-cooked meals, and opportunities to interact with locals and immerse yourself in island traditions.

Island Homestays: For a truly immersive experience, consider staying with a local family in their island home. This intimate and personalized approach to accommodation allows you to forge meaningful connections with your hosts, learn about Maldivian customs and traditions firsthand, and gain insights into island life that you won't find in any guidebook.

4. Budget-Friendly Options:

Shared Accommodations: Travelers on a budget can opt for shared accommodations in dormitory-style rooms or shared houses, which offer affordable rates without compromising on comfort or convenience. These options are ideal for solo travelers, backpackers, and groups looking to stretch their budget while still enjoying the beauty and charm of the Maldives.

No matter which accommodation option you choose, you're sure to find yourself surrounded by breathtaking natural beauty, warm hospitality, and endless opportunities for relaxation and adventure in the Maldives. So whether you're dreaming of a lavish escape in an overwater villa or a cozy retreat in a local guesthouse, your perfect paradise awaits in the jewel-toned waters of the Maldives.

Transportation within the Maldives

Welcome to the Maldives, where turquoise waters, palm-fringed islands, and endless adventures beckon at every turn. As you embark on your journey to this tropical paradise, let's explore the various transportation options that will help you navigate the stunning archipelago with ease and convenience.

1. Seaplanes:

Prepare for a breathtaking aerial adventure as you soar above the Maldives' picturesque atolls in a seaplane. Offering panoramic views of coral reefs, turquoise lagoons, and secluded islands, seaplane transfers provide a scenic and exhilarating way to travel between the main international airport in Male and your chosen resort or island destination.

Seaplanes operate regular scheduled flights to and from numerous resorts and seaplane bases located throughout the Maldives, with flights typically lasting between 15 minutes to an hour depending on the distance.

2. Speedboats:

For travelers seeking a more direct and efficient mode of transportation, speedboats offer a convenient option for navigating the Maldives' crystal-clear waters. Speedboat transfers are available for resorts located within close proximity to the main international airport in Male, providing swift and seamless connections to your island paradise.

Speedboat transfers typically range from 20 minutes to a few hours depending on the distance, with private and shared transfer options available to suit your preferences and budget.

3. Domestic Flights:

Explore the Maldives' diverse array of atolls and islands by taking advantage of the extensive network of domestic flights that connect major hubs and remote island communities throughout the archipelago. Domestic flights operate regularly from the main international airport in Male to domestic airports located on inhabited islands, offering convenient access to popular tourist destinations and off-the-beaten-path gems.

Domestic flights are operated by local airlines and typically last between 20 minutes to an hour depending on the distance, with comfortable and modern aircraft providing a hassle-free travel experience.

4. Ferries:

For budget-conscious travelers and those looking to explore multiple islands at a leisurely pace, ferries offer an affordable and scenic mode of transportation between inhabited islands in the Maldives. Public ferries operate regular scheduled services between Male and various local islands, providing an opportunity to experience authentic Maldivian culture and interact with local communities along the way.

Ferry schedules and routes may vary depending on weather conditions and demand, so it's advisable to check timetables in advance and plan your journey accordingly.

5. Private Yachts and Cruises:

For those seeking the ultimate luxury and freedom to explore the Maldives' hidden treasures at their own pace, private yachts and cruises offer an exclusive and indulgent mode of transportation.

Charter a yacht or book a luxury cruise to sail the Maldives' pristine waters in style, with personalized itineraries tailored to your preferences and desires. Private yachts and cruises provide an unparalleled opportunity to discover secluded beaches, uninhabited islands, and pristine dive sites, with onboard amenities and services ensuring a comfortable and unforgettable journey.

No matter which transportation option you choose, you're sure to be enchanted by the beauty and tranquility of the Maldives as you journey from one idyllic island to the next. So sit back, relax, and let the magic of the Maldives unfold as you explore this tropical paradise like never before.

LOCAL INSIGHTS
Traditional Maldivian cuisine and dining experiences

Prepare your taste buds for a culinary journey unlike any other as we delve into the vibrant and flavorful world of traditional Maldivian cuisine. With influences from India, Sri Lanka, and the Middle East, Maldivian dishes are a celebration of fresh seafood, aromatic spices, and tropical ingredients, offering a tantalizing blend of flavors and textures that will leave you craving more.

1. Fresh Seafood Delicacies:

With its abundant marine resources, it's no surprise that seafood takes center stage in Maldivian cuisine. From succulent grilled fish and fragrant curries to savory fish soups and crispy fried snacks, there's no shortage of ways to enjoy the ocean's bounty in the Maldives.

Must-try dishes include mas riha (spicy fish curry), garudhiya (clear fish broth served with rice), and kulhi boakibaa (fish cake flavored with coconut and spices), each showcasing the depth and diversity of Maldivian seafood cuisine.

2. Coconut-infused Creations:

Coconut is a staple ingredient in Maldivian cooking, adding richness, sweetness, and depth of flavor to many traditional dishes. Coconut milk, grated coconut, and coconut oil are commonly used in curries, stews, and desserts, imparting a distinctive tropical taste to every bite.

Indulge in decadent desserts like bondibai (coconut milk rice pudding), huni hakuru folhi (coconut and jaggery pancakes), and foni boakibaa (coconut cake), each showcasing the versatility and deliciousness of coconut in Maldivian sweets.

3. Spice-infused Sensations:

Maldivian cuisine is known for its bold and aromatic spice blends, which add complexity and depth to dishes while tantalizing the senses with their fragrant aromas. Common spices used in Maldivian cooking include curry leaves, cinnamon, cardamom, cloves, and chili peppers, each lending its own unique flavor profile to traditional dishes.

Sample spicy delights like mas huni (a fiery blend of shredded tuna, coconut, onions, and chili), rihaakuru (a savory fish paste used as a condiment), and rihaakuru roshi (a spicy tuna and chili paste served with flatbread), each showcasing the bold and flavorful spices of Maldivian cuisine.

4. Dining Experiences:

Sunset Dinners: Experience the magic of a Maldivian sunset with a romantic beachfront dinner, where you'll dine al fresco under a canopy of stars while savoring fresh seafood and tropical delicacies.

Traditional Bodu Beru: Immerse yourself in the rhythmic beats and infectious energy of a bodu beru performance, a traditional Maldivian drumming ensemble that accompanies festive gatherings and celebrations, often accompanied by feasting and merriment.

Cultural Cooking Classes: Delve into the heart of Maldivian culture with a hands-on cooking class, where you'll learn to prepare authentic dishes using traditional techniques and locally sourced ingredients, all under the guidance of knowledgeable chefs and home cooks.

From the tantalizing flavors of fresh seafood to the aromatic spices and tropical ingredients that define Maldivian cuisine, every bite is a journey of discovery and delight in this island paradise. So come hungry, leave satisfied, and savor the flavors of paradise with every unforgettable dining experience in the Maldives.

Cultural etiquette and customs

As you set foot on the sun-kissed shores of the Maldives, you're not just embarking on a journey to paradise; you're also stepping into a world rich in history, tradition, and culture. To ensure your visit is as enriching and respectful as possible, let's explore some key cultural etiquette and customs that will help you navigate this captivating destination with grace and sensitivity.

1. Respect for Islam:

Islam is the official religion of the Maldives, and religious customs and practices hold significant importance in daily life. Visitors should be mindful of local sensitivities and show respect for Islamic traditions, such as modest dress and behavior, particularly when visiting religious sites or interacting with locals.

Avoid public displays of affection, excessive drinking, or engaging in behavior that may be considered disrespectful or offensive to Islamic values.

2. Greetings and Courtesy:

Politeness and respect are highly valued in Maldivian culture, and greetings play an important role in social interactions. When meeting someone for the first time, it's customary to offer a warm smile and a handshake, followed by a respectful greeting such as "Assalaamu Alaikum" (peace be upon you).

Use titles and honorifics when addressing elders or individuals in positions of authority, and always speak in a calm and courteous manner, even in challenging situations.

3. Community and Hospitality:

Maldivians are known for their hospitality and generosity, and visitors can expect to be warmly welcomed into homes and communities throughout the islands. Embrace this spirit of hospitality by reciprocating kindness, showing appreciation for local customs, and engaging with locals in a respectful and meaningful way.

If invited to someone's home for a meal or

gathering, bring a small gift as a token of appreciation, such as fruit, sweets, or a bouquet of flowers. Remove your shoes before entering the home and follow the lead of your hosts in terms of dining etiquette and customs.

4. Environmental Conservation:

The Maldives is home to fragile ecosystems and vulnerable marine life, and sustainable practices are essential for preserving the natural beauty of the islands for future generations. Respect the environment by disposing of waste responsibly, conserving water and energy, and supporting eco-friendly initiatives and activities during your visit.

When engaging in water sports or marine activities, adhere to guidelines for responsible snorkeling, diving, and wildlife viewing to minimize impact on coral reefs and marine habitats.

5. Cultural Sensitivity:

Be mindful of cultural sensitivities and customs when exploring local communities and interacting with residents. Seek permission before taking photographs of individuals or sacred sites, and refrain from intrusive or disrespectful behavior that may infringe upon personal privacy or cultural traditions.

Educate yourself about Maldivian culture, history, and customs before your trip, and approach cultural experiences with an open mind and a willingness to learn and engage respectfully with local traditions and practices.

By embracing the cultural etiquette and customs of the Maldives with sensitivity and respect, you'll not only enrich your travel experience but also forge meaningful connections with the vibrant communities and traditions that make this island nation so special. Soak in the beauty of the Maldives, both above and below the surface, and leave a positive and lasting impression as you journey through this enchanting destination.

Insider tips for experiencing local life

While the Maldives is renowned for its luxurious resorts and pristine beaches, there's much more to discover beyond the tourist hotspots. To truly experience the essence of Maldivian culture and lifestyle, consider these insider tips that will help you connect with local communities, traditions, and hidden gems off the beaten path.

1. Venture Beyond the Resorts:

While the allure of overwater bungalows and private beaches is undeniable, don't miss the opportunity to explore local islands and communities. Take a day trip to nearby inhabited islands, where you can wander through colorful markets, interact with friendly locals, and sample authentic Maldivian cuisine at local cafes and eateries.

2. Embrace Homestays and Guesthouses:

For a more immersive experience, consider staying in a local guesthouse or homestay on one of the inhabited islands. These accommodations offer a unique opportunity to live like a local, sharing meals with your hosts, learning about Maldivian customs and traditions, and participating in daily life activities such as fishing, cooking, or weaving.

3. Connect with Locals:

Strike up conversations with locals you encounter during your travels, whether it's a friendly fisherman casting his net or a group of children playing on the beach. Maldivians are known for their warmth and hospitality, and you'll find that many are eager to share their stories, traditions, and recommendations for hidden gems in their community.

4. Explore Cultural Events and Festivals:

Keep an eye out for cultural events and festivals taking place during your visit, such as Bodu Eid (Eid al-Fitr), Eid al-Adha, or the annual Maldives Fishermen's Day. These celebrations offer a fascinating glimpse into

Maldivian culture and heritage, with traditional music, dance, food, and festivities that bring communities together in joyful celebration.

5. Support Local Artisans and Craftspeople:

Seek out local artisans and craftspeople who create traditional Maldivian handicrafts such as lacquerware, mat weaving, and wood carving. Visit local workshops and markets to purchase authentic souvenirs and support the livelihoods of talented artisans who keep these ancient crafts alive.

6. Participate in Community Activities:

Keep an eye out for community activities and initiatives that welcome visitor participation, such as coral reef restoration projects, beach cleanups, or cultural workshops. Not only will you contribute to meaningful causes, but you'll also have the opportunity to engage with locals and forge lasting connections with the community.

7. Learn Basic Phrases in Dhivehi:

While English is widely spoken in the Maldives, learning a few basic phrases in Dhivehi, the local language, can go a long way in fostering rapport and building relationships with locals. Practice greetings, expressions of gratitude, and simple conversational phrases to enhance your interactions and show appreciation for Maldivian culture.

By embracing these insider tips for experiencing local life in the Maldives, you'll unlock a world of authentic experiences, cultural insights, and meaningful connections that will enrich your journey and leave you with memories to cherish for a lifetime. So step off the beaten path, immerse yourself in the vibrant tapestry of Maldivian culture, and embark on an unforgettable adventure beyond the resorts and beaches.

Recommended off-the-beaten-path destinations

Beyond the well-trodden paths of the luxury resorts and tourist hubs, lies a world of hidden gems waiting to be discovered in the Maldives. For travelers seeking to escape the crowds and delve deeper into the authentic beauty of the archipelago, here are some off-the-beaten-path destinations that promise unforgettable experiences and unparalleled adventures.

1. Fuvahmulah:

Tucked away in the southernmost reaches of the Maldives, Fuvahmulah is a secluded paradise renowned for its unique geography and rich biodiversity. Unlike the typical coral atolls that define much of the Maldives, Fuvahmulah boasts a striking landscape of lush greenery, freshwater lakes, and rugged cliffs, earning it the nickname "the Island of the Areca Nut."

Explore the island's pristine beaches, venture into its dense mangrove forests, and discover hidden waterfalls and natural pools tucked away in the heart of the island. Fuvahmulah is also a haven for birdwatchers, with over 100 species of birds inhabiting its diverse ecosystems.

2. Addu Atoll:

Located in the southernmost region of the Maldives, Addu Atoll offers a tranquil retreat far removed from the hustle and bustle of the more touristy islands. Comprising six inhabited islands and numerous uninhabited islets, Addu Atoll is a paradise for nature lovers and outdoor enthusiasts.

Explore the untouched beauty of Addu Atoll's coral reefs, where vibrant marine life thrives in crystal-clear waters teeming with colorful fish, sea turtles, and reef sharks. Embark on a cycling adventure along the scenic coastline, passing through sleepy fishing villages, lush coconut groves, and historical landmarks dating back to World War II.

3. Hulhudhoo Island:

Nestled within the Gaafu Alifu Atoll,

Hulhudhoo Island offers a serene and unspoiled escape for travelers seeking solitude and tranquility. With its pristine beaches, swaying palm trees, and turquoise lagoons, Hulhudhoo epitomizes the idyllic beauty of the Maldives.

Immerse yourself in the local way of life by visiting the island's bustling fishing harbor, where colorful dhoni boats unload their daily catch of fresh seafood. Wander through the narrow streets of the village, where children play in the shade of coconut palms and locals go about their daily routines with a quiet sense of contentment.

4. Thoddoo Island:

Known as the breadbasket of the Maldives, Thoddoo Island is renowned for its thriving agriculture industry, particularly its abundant production of watermelons and other tropical fruits. Tucked away in the Alif Alif Atoll, Thoddoo offers a tranquil escape from the tourist crowds, with pristine beaches, lush orchards, and charming guesthouses.

Explore the island's verdant interior on foot or bicycle, stopping to admire the colorful fruit orchards and lush fields of watermelon, papaya, and banana. Take a refreshing dip in the crystal-clear waters of Thoddoo's beaches, where you can snorkel among vibrant coral reefs and encounter a dazzling array of marine life.

5. Maafushi Island:

While Maafushi has gained popularity in recent years as a budget-friendly destination with a burgeoning guesthouse industry, it still retains much of its local charm and authenticity. Located in the Kaafu Atoll, Maafushi offers a mix of pristine beaches, cultural experiences, and outdoor adventures.

Discover Maafushi's rich cultural heritage by visiting the island's mosque, museum, and traditional handicraft shops, where you can learn about Maldivian art, history, and craftsmanship. Explore the surrounding waters on a snorkeling or diving excursion, where you'll encounter vibrant coral reefs, playful dolphins, and majestic whale sharks.

Venture off the beaten path in the Maldives, and you'll discover a world of hidden treasures waiting to be explored. From secluded islands and pristine beaches to vibrant coral reefs and cultural experiences, these off-the-beaten-path destinations promise unforgettable adventures and authentic encounters that will leave you with memories to last a lifetime. So pack your bags, leave the crowds behind, and embark on a journey of discovery in the breathtaking Maldives.

EXPLORING THE ISLANDS

Popular tourist islands and attractions

Welcome to the Maldives, where every island is a postcard-perfect paradise waiting to be explored. From the iconic atolls of North Male to the pristine shores of Addu City, each destination offers its own unique blend of natural beauty, cultural experiences, and outdoor adventures. Let's embark on a journey to discover some of the most popular tourist islands and attractions that make the Maldives a dream destination for travelers from around the world.

1. North Male Atoll:

Home to the capital city of Male, North Male Atoll is the gateway to the Maldives and a hub of cultural and historical attractions. Explore the bustling streets of Male, where colorful markets, historic mosques, and lively cafes offer a glimpse into daily life in the Maldives. Don't miss iconic landmarks such as the Grand Friday Mosque, Sultan Park, and the bustling fish market.

2. South Male Atoll:

South Male Atoll is renowned for its picture-perfect beaches, vibrant coral reefs, and luxurious resorts. Discover the underwater wonders of sites like Banana Reef and Kuda Giri Shipwreck, where colorful coral gardens and diverse marine life await snorkelers and divers alike. For a taste of local culture, visit nearby inhabited islands like Guraidhoo and Maafushi, where you can interact with friendly locals and experience authentic Maldivian hospitality.

3. Ari Atoll:

As one of the largest atolls in the Maldives, Ari Atoll offers a wealth of attractions for nature lovers and adventure seekers. Dive into the crystal-clear waters of Maaya Thila and Fish Head, two of the Maldives' most famous dive sites, where encounters with reef sharks, manta rays, and whale sharks are virtually guaranteed. Back on land, explore the laid-back vibe of islands like Dhigurah and Dhangethi, where pristine beaches and lush coconut groves await.

4. Baa Atoll:

Baa Atoll is a UNESCO Biosphere Reserve renowned for its rich biodiversity and stunning natural landscapes. Dive into the heart of the atoll at Hanifaru Bay, a marine sanctuary famous for its annual gathering of manta rays and whale sharks. Explore the mangrove forests and coral reefs of Fulhadhoo Island, or embark on a snorkeling adventure at the vibrant reef gardens of Dhigali Haa.

5. Addu City:

Located in the southernmost region of the Maldives, Addu City offers a tranquil retreat far removed from the tourist crowds. Explore the historic landmarks of Gan Island, including the British Loyalty Memorial and the remnants of a World War II-era British naval base. Cycle along the scenic coastline of Hithadhoo Island, or unwind on the pristine beaches of Maradhoo and Hulhudhoo.

6. Hulhumale Island:

Developed as a reclaimed island adjacent to Male, Hulhumale offers a modern and cosmopolitan vibe with a range of attractions and amenities. Relax on the island's spacious beaches, take a stroll along the picturesque waterfront promenade, or enjoy water sports and activities such as kayaking, jet skiing, and parasailing. Don't miss the opportunity to sample local cuisine at the island's restaurants and cafes, where fresh seafood and traditional Maldivian dishes are served with a contemporary twist.

From the vibrant streets of Male to the pristine shores of Addu City, the Maldives offers a wealth of attractions and experiences for every type of traveler. Whether you're seeking adventure, relaxation, or cultural immersion, these popular tourist islands and attractions are sure to captivate your imagination and leave you with memories to last a lifetime. So pack your bags, prepare for paradise, and embark on the journey of a lifetime in the breathtaking Maldives.

Water activities (snorkeling, diving, surfing, etc.)

Welcome to a world where crystal-clear waters, vibrant coral reefs, and an abundance of marine life beckon you to dive in and explore. In the Maldives, water activities aren't just pastimes—they're opportunities to immerse yourself in the breathtaking beauty of the Indian Ocean and create unforgettable memories that will last a lifetime. Let's dive into some of the most exhilarating water activities that await you in this tropical paradise.

1. Snorkeling:

Grab your mask, snorkel, and fins, and get ready to discover a kaleidoscope of colors beneath the surface of the ocean. The Maldives is renowned for its pristine coral reefs, teeming with a dazzling array of marine life, including colorful fish, graceful sea turtles, and majestic manta rays. Whether you're snorkeling off the shore of your resort or exploring remote reef systems, the underwater world of the Maldives is sure to leave you in awe.

2. Diving:

Strap on your scuba gear and prepare for an adventure into the depths of the Indian Ocean, where a world of wonders awaits beneath the surface. With dive sites ranging from shallow coral gardens to deep underwater pinnacles, the Maldives offers something for divers of all skill levels. Explore vibrant coral reefs teeming with fish, drift along underwater currents with graceful sharks and rays, or marvel at the intricate wrecks and caves that dot the ocean floor.

3. Surfing:

With its pristine waves and uncrowded breaks, the Maldives is a paradise for surfers seeking the perfect wave. Whether you're a seasoned pro or a novice looking to catch your first break, the Maldives offers a variety of surf spots to suit every skill level and preference. From the legendary waves of North Male Atoll to the hidden gems of Addu City, you'll find endless opportunities to ride the waves and experience the thrill of surfing in paradise.

4. Stand-Up Paddleboarding (SUP):

Experience the tranquility of gliding across the surface of the ocean on a stand-up paddleboard (SUP), where you can enjoy panoramic views of the surrounding islands and marine life below. Whether you're exploring calm lagoons, paddling through mangrove forests, or embarking on sunset tours, SUP offers a fun and relaxing way to connect with nature and soak in the beauty of the Maldives from a unique perspective.

5. Jet Skiing and Water Sports:

For adrenaline junkies and thrill-seekers, jet

skiing, parasailing, and other water sports offer an exhilarating way to experience the Maldives' pristine waters. Zoom across the ocean on a high-speed jet ski, soar above the waves on a parasail, or try your hand at windsurfing, kiteboarding, or wakeboarding for an action-packed day on the water.

6. Dolphin Watching and Sunset Cruises:

Set sail on a sunset cruise or dolphin-watching excursion and experience the magic of the Maldives' coastal waters as the sun dips below the horizon. Keep an eye out for playful dolphins frolicking in the waves, or simply sit back, relax, and savor the beauty of the Maldivian sunset as you cruise along the tranquil waters of the Indian Ocean.

Whether you're snorkeling among vibrant coral reefs, riding the waves on a surfboard, or embarking on a sunset cruise, water activities in the Maldives offer endless opportunities for adventure, relaxation, and unforgettable experiences. So pack your swimsuit, sunscreen, and sense of adventure, and get ready to dive into the aquatic playground of paradise in the breathtaking Maldives.

Land activities (sightseeing, hiking, etc.)

While the Maldives is renowned for its stunning beaches and pristine waters, the islands also offer a wealth of land-based activities that promise adventure, cultural immersion, and unforgettable experiences. From exploring lush tropical landscapes to discovering historical landmarks and local communities, there's something for every traveler to enjoy on land in this tropical paradise. Let's dive into some of the top land activities that await you in the Maldives.

1. Island Hopping:

Embark on a journey of discovery as you hop from one idyllic island to the next, exploring the unique charm and beauty of each destination. Whether you're visiting inhabited islands to immerse yourself in local culture and traditions or venturing to uninhabited islets for secluded picnics and beachcombing adventures, island hopping offers a fascinating glimpse into the diverse landscapes and lifestyles of the Maldives.

2. Sightseeing and Cultural Tours:

Dive into the rich history and heritage of the Maldives with sightseeing and cultural tours that take you to historical landmarks, ancient ruins, and traditional villages. Explore the vibrant streets of Male, the capital city, where you can visit historic sites such as the Old Friday Mosque, Mulee Aage Palace, and the National Museum, which houses a fascinating collection of artifacts and exhibits showcasing Maldivian history and culture.

3. Nature Walks and Hiking:

Lace up your hiking boots and set out to explore the natural beauty of the Maldives on foot, with nature walks and hiking trails that lead you through lush tropical forests, verdant valleys, and scenic viewpoints. Trek to the summit of islands like Hulhumale, where panoramic vistas of the surrounding atolls and ocean await, or explore the mangrove forests and bird sanctuaries of islands like Viligili and Hithadhoo.

4. Birdwatching and Wildlife Encounters:

The Maldives is home to a diverse array of bird species, including colorful migratory birds and endemic species found nowhere else on earth. Grab your binoculars and embark on a birdwatching adventure in the wetlands and mangroves of islands like Gan and Fuvahmulah, where you can spot herons, egrets, kingfishers, and more in their natural habitat. Keep an eye out for other wildlife encounters, including sightings of sea turtles, dolphins, and even elusive whale sharks.

5. Cultural Experiences and Workshops:

Immerse yourself in Maldivian culture and traditions with hands-on experiences and workshops that offer insights into local customs, crafts, and cuisine. Learn to weave traditional mats and baskets from coconut leaves, try your hand at Maldivian cooking with a culinary class featuring local ingredients and recipes, or participate in cultural performances and ceremonies that celebrate the vibrant heritage of the islands.

6. Sunset and Stargazing:

End your day on a magical note with sunset and stargazing experiences that showcase the breathtaking beauty of the Maldivian sky. Whether you're enjoying a romantic sunset cruise, lounging on the beach with a cocktail in hand, or stargazing from the deck of your overwater villa, the Maldives offers some of the most spectacular sunsets and night skies you'll ever witness.

From island hopping and sightseeing tours to nature walks and cultural workshops, land activities in the Maldives offer a wealth of opportunities for exploration, adventure, and cultural immersion. So step off the beach, lace up your shoes, and get ready to discover the hidden treasures and natural wonders that await you on land in this enchanting destination.

Wildlife encounters (marine life, bird watching, etc.)

In the Maldives, nature isn't just a backdrop—it's a vibrant and thriving ecosystem teeming with diverse marine life, exotic birds, and breathtaking wildlife encounters waiting to be discovered. From the colorful coral reefs of the Indian Ocean to the lush mangrove forests and wetlands of the islands, the Maldives offers a playground for wildlife enthusiasts and nature lovers alike. Let's dive into some of the most captivating wildlife encounters that await you in this tropical paradise.

1. Snorkeling with Marine Life:

Strap on your mask and fins and prepare for an underwater adventure like no other as you snorkel among the vibrant coral reefs and tropical fish of the Maldives. From the dazzling colors of parrotfish and butterflyfish to the graceful movements of sea turtles and eagle rays, every snorkeling excursion offers a chance to encounter a mesmerizing array of marine life in their natural habitat.

2. Diving with Sharks and Rays:

For adrenaline junkies and thrill-seekers, diving in the Maldives offers the opportunity to come face-to-face with some of the ocean's most majestic predators, including sharks and rays. Dive sites like Maaya Thila and Fish Head are renowned for their resident populations of reef sharks, while manta ray cleaning stations in sites like Hanifaru Bay provide unforgettable encounters with these gentle giants of the sea.

3. Dolphin Watching:

Set sail on a dolphin-watching excursion and witness the playful antics of spinner dolphins as they leap and frolic in the wake of your boat. With their acrobatic displays and sociable nature, spinner dolphins are a common sight in the waters surrounding the Maldives, offering plenty of opportunities for memorable encounters and photo opportunities.

4. Birdwatching in Wetlands and Mangroves:

The Maldives is a paradise for birdwatchers, with its lush mangrove forests, wetlands, and coastal habitats providing sanctuary for a diverse array of bird species. Grab your binoculars and explore birdwatching hotspots like Hithadhoo Island, where you can spot herons, egrets, kingfishers, and other migratory and endemic birds in their natural habitat.

5. Turtle Nesting and Hatchling Releases:

Experience the wonder of nature up close with a visit to a sea turtle nesting site, where you can witness these ancient creatures coming ashore to lay their eggs under the cover of darkness. If you're lucky, you may even have the opportunity to participate in a turtle hatchling release, where baby turtles make their journey from the nest to the sea for the first time, guided by the light of the moon.

6. Whale Shark Encounters:

The Maldives is one of the best places in the world to encounter whale sharks, the largest fish in the ocean, in their natural habitat. Join a guided snorkeling or diving excursion to renowned whale shark hotspots like South Ari Atoll or Baa Atoll, where you can swim alongside these gentle giants and marvel at their immense size and graceful movements.

From snorkeling among colorful coral reefs to witnessing the majestic beauty of whale sharks and manta rays, wildlife encounters in the Maldives offer a thrilling and unforgettable glimpse into the wonders of the natural world. So pack your camera, binoculars, and sense of adventure, and get ready to embark on a wildlife adventure of a lifetime in this breathtaking tropical paradise.

CRAFTING YOUR PERFECT MALDIVES ITINERARY

In the heart of the Indian Ocean lies a destination that epitomizes paradise—welcome to the Maldives. With its powder-white beaches, crystal-clear waters, and vibrant coral reefs, this island nation beckons travelers from around the globe to experience its unparalleled beauty and tranquility. Crafting the perfect itinerary allows you to immerse yourself in the wonders of the Maldives, whether you're seeking relaxation, adventure, romance, or family fun. Let's delve into the possibilities and create an itinerary that will make your Maldives getaway truly unforgettable.

Unwind in Island Bliss

Day 1: Arrival in Paradise

Your journey begins as you touch down in the Maldives, greeted by the warm tropical breeze and the promise of adventure. Transfer to your chosen island resort, where you'll be welcomed with a refreshing drink and a warm smile. Settle into your luxurious accommodation, whether it's an overwater villa, beachfront bungalow, or secluded hideaway nestled amidst lush foliage.

Day 2: Beachfront Bliss

Wake up to the gentle sound of waves lapping against the shore and step outside to witness the breathtaking beauty of your island paradise. Spend the day unwinding on the pristine beaches, sinking your toes into the soft sand, and basking in the warm tropical sun. Indulge in a leisurely breakfast served in the privacy of your villa, savoring tropical fruits, freshly baked pastries, and exotic juices.

Day 3: Spa Sanctuary

Treat yourself to a day of pampering and relaxation at the resort's world-class spa. Choose from an array of rejuvenating treatments inspired by ancient healing traditions, from soothing massages and body scrubs to revitalizing facials and holistic therapies. Let the stresses of everyday life melt away as you surrender to the healing touch of expert therapists and the tranquil surroundings of the spa sanctuary.

Day 4: Sunset Serenade

As the sun begins to dip below the horizon, embark on a sunset cruise aboard a traditional dhoni boat. Sail across the calm waters of the Indian Ocean, sipping champagne and savoring canapes as you watch the sky ignite in a blaze of colors. Toast to the beauty of the moment with your loved one, creating memories that will last a lifetime.

Dive into Underwater Wonderland

Day 1: Arrival and Dive Briefing

Arrive in the Maldives and transfer to your chosen dive resort or liveaboard vessel. Attend a dive briefing to familiarize yourself with the diving procedures, safety protocols, and the incredible underwater world that awaits. Meet your dive guides and fellow divers, sharing stories and excitement for the adventures ahead.

Day 2: Explore Vibrant Reefs

Dive into the crystal-clear waters of the Maldives to explore vibrant coral reefs teeming with life. Encounter colorful reef fish darting among coral formations, graceful sea turtles gliding through the water, and majestic manta rays soaring overhead. Dive at iconic sites such as Maaya Thila, Kandooma Thila, and Fish Head, where the underwater scenery is nothing short of spectacular.

Day 3: Encounters with Giants

Embark on a special excursion to encounter some of the Maldives' most magnificent marine creatures, including whale sharks and manta rays. Join a guided snorkeling or diving excursion to hotspots such as Hanifaru Bay or the South Ari Atoll, where these gentle giants gather in large numbers to feed and socialize. Witness the awe-inspiring sight of these majestic creatures up close, their graceful movements leaving a lasting impression.

Day 4: Dive Safari Adventure

Embark on a dive safari adventure to explore remote atolls, pristine reefs, and hidden underwater gems. Set sail aboard a liveaboard vessel equipped with all the amenities for a comfortable and unforgettable diving experience. Dive at multiple sites throughout the day, encountering a diverse array of marine life and exploring untouched underwater landscapes. Relax on deck between dives, soaking up the sun and exchanging stories with fellow divers from around the world.

Family-Friendly Fun in the Sun

Day 1: Island Arrival and Family Bonding

Arrive in the Maldives and transfer to your chosen family-friendly resort or beachfront villa. Settle into your spacious accommodation and spend the day bonding with your loved ones amidst the natural beauty of the island. Build sandcastles on the beach, splash in the shallows, and embark on a family treasure hunt to explore the island's hidden secrets.

Day 2: Marine Discovery

Embark on a family-friendly snorkeling adventure to discover the wonders of the underwater world.

Explore colorful coral reefs, swim alongside tropical fish, and search for playful dolphins frolicking in the waves. Opt for a glass-bottom boat tour for younger children or those not comfortable with snorkeling, providing a window into the vibrant marine ecosystem below.

Day 3: Island Exploration and Cultural Immersion

Venture beyond the resort to explore a local Maldivian island and immerse yourselves in the rich culture and traditions of the archipelago. Visit traditional villages, learn about local customs and crafts, and sample authentic Maldivian cuisine at a local restaurant. Engage in cultural activities such as coconut palm weaving, drumming, or traditional dance performances, creating lasting memories for the whole family.

Day 4: Family Fun and Adventure

Spend the day enjoying a variety of family-friendly activities and adventures, from water sports and beach games to nature walks and wildlife encounters. Take advantage of the resort's children's clubs, supervised activities, and family-friendly amenities, ensuring that every member of the family has a memorable and enjoyable experience. End the day with a family barbecue on the beach, sharing stories and laughter under the starlit sky.

Adventure Seeker's Expedition

Day 1: Arrival and Thrilling Adventures

Arrive in the Maldives and kick off your adrenaline-fueled adventure with a day of thrilling water sports and activities. Try your hand at windsurfing, parasailing, or jet skiing, or embark on a guided snorkeling safari to explore remote reefs and underwater caves. Feel the rush of excitement as you dive into the crystal-clear waters and discover the wonders that lie beneath the surface.

Day 2: Surfing Safari

Head to one of the Maldives' renowned surf breaks for a day of epic waves and unforgettable surf sessions. Whether you're a seasoned pro or a novice surfer, the Maldives offers waves for every skill level, with expert instructors available to provide guidance and support. Ride the waves, feel the adrenaline pumping through your veins, and experience the thrill of surfing in paradise.

Day 3: Island Exploration and Adventure

Embark on an island-hopping adventure to discover the Maldives' hidden gems and off-the-beaten-path destinations. Explore uninhabited islands, pristine lagoons, and secluded beaches, with opportunities for snorkeling, picnicking, and wildlife encounters along the way. Take a guided nature hike through lush tropical forests, spotting exotic wildlife and bird species as you explore the natural beauty of the islands.

Day 4: Sunset Fishing Excursion and Nightlife

Conclude your adventure-packed itinerary with a sunset fishing excursion aboard a traditional Maldivian dhoni. Cast your line and try your luck at catching the evening's dinner, then return to shore to enjoy a seafood feast at a beachfront restaurant. As night falls, experience the vibrant nightlife of the Maldives, with live music, cultural performances, and beachside bonfires lighting up the night sky.

Crafting your perfect Maldives itinerary is a journey of discovery, adventure, and relaxation—an opportunity to create unforgettable memories and experience the magic of this tropical paradise. Whether you're seeking romance, family fun, underwater exploration, or adrenaline-fueled adventures, the Maldives offers endless possibilities for every type of traveler. So pack your bags, prepare for the adventure of a lifetime, and let the beauty of the Maldives captivate your heart and soul.

PHOTOGRAPHY TIPS
Capturing the beauty of the Maldives

In the Maldives, every sunset is a masterpiece, every coral reef a kaleidoscope of colors, and every palm-fringed island a postcard-perfect paradise waiting to be captured through the lens of your camera. With its pristine beaches, crystal-clear waters, and vibrant marine life, the Maldives offers endless opportunities for photographers to create stunning images that capture the essence of this breathtaking destination. Here are some tips to help you make the most of your photographic journey in the Maldives.

1. Chase the Light:

The golden hours of sunrise and sunset cast a magical glow over the Maldivian landscape, bathing everything in warm, soft light that enhances colors and textures. Wake up early to catch the first light of dawn painting the sky in hues of pink and orange, or stay out late to capture the dramatic hues of sunset reflecting off the water. Experiment with different angles and compositions to make the most of these magical moments.

2. Explore Underwater Photography:

With its crystal-clear waters and diverse marine life, the Maldives is a paradise for underwater photographers. Invest in a waterproof camera or housing and explore the vibrant coral reefs, underwater pinnacles, and marine ecosystems that teem with colorful fish, sea turtles, and other exotic creatures. Experiment with different settings and techniques to capture the beauty of the underwater world in all its glory.

3. Capture Local Life and Culture:

Beyond the beaches and resorts, the Maldives is home to a rich tapestry of culture and traditions waiting to be discovered through your lens. Venture into local villages, markets, and fishing harbors to capture authentic moments of daily life, from children playing in the sand to fishermen hauling in their catch of the day. Engage with locals, ask permission before taking photos, and respect their privacy and customs.

4. Experiment with Aerial Photography:

Take your photography to new heights with aerial shots that offer a unique perspective of the Maldivian islands from above. Whether you're flying in a seaplane, helicopter, or drone, aerial photography allows you to capture sweeping panoramas of islands, atolls, and lagoons that showcase the breathtaking beauty and natural diversity of the Maldives from a bird's-eye view.

5. Focus on Details and Textures:

In addition to sweeping landscapes and iconic landmarks, don't forget to zoom in on the details and textures that make the Maldives so special. From the intricate patterns of coral reefs and shells to the delicate hues of tropical flowers and foliage, there's beauty to be found in every corner of this tropical paradise. Experiment with macro photography to capture the tiny wonders that often go unnoticed.

6. Embrace Weather and Elements:

The weather in the Maldives can be unpredictable, with sudden rain showers and passing clouds adding drama and texture to your photos. Embrace the elements and use them to your advantage, capturing the contrast between sunlight and shadow, or the reflections of clouds in calm lagoons. Don't be afraid to get wet or sandy to capture that perfect shot—it's all part of the adventure.

7. Tell a Story with Your Photos:

Ultimately, photography is about more than just capturing beautiful images—it's about telling a story and evoking emotions through your photos. Whether you're documenting your own travel experiences, showcasing the natural beauty of the Maldives, or highlighting the resilience and vibrancy of local communities, let your photos speak for themselves and share the magic of the Maldives with the world.

With its stunning natural beauty, vibrant culture, and endless opportunities for adventure and exploration, the Maldives is a photographer's paradise just waiting to be discovered. So pack your camera, pack your sense of wonder, and get ready to capture the beauty of paradise in every frame.

Best times of day for photography

In the Maldives, where every sunrise and sunset is a masterpiece waiting to be captured, timing is everything when it comes to photography. From the soft, golden light of dawn to the vibrant hues of sunset, the Maldives offers endless opportunities for photographers to create stunning images that showcase the beauty of this tropical paradise. Let's explore the best times of day for photography in the Maldives and how to make the most of each magical moment.

1. Sunrise:

There's something truly magical about the early hours of the morning when the world is just waking up and the sky is painted in hues of pink, orange, and gold. Set your alarm and head out before dawn to capture the first light of sunrise as it bathes the landscape in a warm, soft glow. Whether you're photographing the silhouette of palm trees against the horizon or the reflections of the sky in calm, glassy waters, sunrise in the Maldives is a time of breathtaking beauty and tranquility.

2. Mid-Morning:

As the sun rises higher in the sky, the light becomes harsher and more intense, making it challenging to capture subtle details and textures in your photos. However, mid-morning is still a great time for photography, especially if you're shooting landscapes or seascapes where the harsh light can create dramatic shadows and contrast. Experiment with different angles and compositions to make the most of the light and capture unique perspectives of the Maldivian landscape.

3. Afternoon:

In the heat of the afternoon, when the sun is at its peak, it's best to seek shade or take a break from photography to avoid harsh shadows and overexposed images. However, as the afternoon progresses and the sun begins to dip lower in the sky, the light becomes softer and more flattering, creating ideal conditions for capturing portraits, wildlife, and close-up details. Look for interesting subjects and compositions that are illuminated by the warm, golden light of late afternoon.

4. Sunset:

Sunset is undoubtedly the most magical time of day for photography in the Maldives, as the sky ignites in a symphony of colors and the world is bathed in a soft, golden glow. Whether you're photographing silhouettes of palm trees against the fiery sky or reflections of the sunset in the tranquil waters, sunset offers endless opportunities for capturing breathtaking images that showcase the beauty of paradise in all its glory. Be sure to arrive early to scout out the perfect vantage point and plan your compositions in advance, as the fleeting moments of sunset pass all too quickly.

5. Blue Hour:

After the sun has dipped below the horizon and twilight sets in, the sky takes on a deep, velvety blue hue known as the "blue hour." This magical time of day offers a unique opportunity for capturing atmospheric and ethereal images, with soft, diffused light that accentuates the colors and textures of the landscape. Whether you're photographing the twinkling lights of a distant island or the stars shining overhead, blue hour is a time of enchantment and wonder that is not to be missed by photographers.

In the Maldives, every moment of the day offers its own unique beauty and opportunities for photography, from the soft, golden light of sunrise to the vibrant hues of sunset and the atmospheric glow of blue hour. So pack your camera, set your alarm, and get ready to capture the magic of paradise in every frame.

Recommended camera equipment

In a destination as breathtakingly beautiful as the Maldives, capturing the essence of paradise requires more than just a smartphone camera—it demands the right gear to help you make the most of every stunning moment. Whether you're a seasoned professional or an enthusiastic amateur, having the right camera equipment can make all the difference in creating unforgettable images that showcase the beauty of this tropical paradise. Here's a guide to the recommended camera equipment for photographing the Maldives.

1. DSLR or Mirrorless Camera:

While smartphones are convenient for capturing quick snapshots, a DSLR or mirrorless camera offers greater control over settings, image quality, and versatility for capturing stunning landscapes, portraits, and wildlife encounters. Look for a camera with a high-resolution sensor, weather-sealed body, and interchangeable lenses to adapt to a variety of shooting conditions in the Maldives.

2. Wide-Angle Lens:

The Maldives is renowned for its expansive seascapes, pristine beaches, and panoramic vistas, making a wide-angle lens an essential tool for capturing the vastness and beauty of the islands. A wide-angle lens allows you to capture sweeping landscapes, dramatic skies, and immersive underwater scenes with greater depth and perspective, ideal for showcasing the natural beauty of paradise.

3. Telephoto Lens:

For capturing close-up details, wildlife encounters, and distant subjects, a telephoto lens is essential for bringing distant scenes closer and isolating subjects against blurred backgrounds. Look for a telephoto lens with a long focal length and fast autofocus capabilities to capture crisp, detailed images of marine life, birds, and other wildlife in the Maldives.

4. Underwater Camera or Housing:

With its crystal-clear waters and vibrant marine life, the Maldives offers endless opportunities for underwater photography. Invest in a waterproof camera or underwater housing for your DSLR or mirrorless camera to capture stunning images of coral reefs, tropical fish, and other aquatic creatures in their natural habitat. Look for a camera with manual exposure controls, fast autofocus, and a wide-angle lens to capture sharp, colorful images underwater.

5. Tripod:

A sturdy tripod is essential for achieving sharp, stable images, especially in low-light conditions such as sunrise, sunset, and blue hour. Look for a lightweight yet durable tripod that is easy to transport and set up on sandy beaches, rocky shores, or uneven terrain in the Maldives. A tripod also allows you to experiment with long exposures for capturing silky-smooth waterfalls, star trails, and night sky photography.

6. Polarizing Filter:

A polarizing filter is a must-have accessory for reducing glare, enhancing colors, and improving contrast in your photos, particularly when shooting landscapes, seascapes, and reflections in the water. Look for a high-quality polarizing filter that fits your lens diameter and allows you to adjust the intensity of polarization to achieve the desired effect in your photos.

7. Waterproof Bag or Case:

Protect your camera gear from the elements with a waterproof bag or case that keeps your equipment safe and dry while exploring the beaches, islands, and underwater environments of the Maldives. Look for a durable, waterproof bag with padded compartments and adjustable straps for carrying your camera, lenses, and accessories comfortably and securely during your adventures.

With the right camera equipment at your disposal, you'll be well-equipped to capture the beauty of paradise in all its glory and create stunning images that showcase the natural wonders of the Maldives. So, pack your gear, prepare for adventure, and get ready to embark on a photographic journey of a lifetime in this tropical paradise.

Editing and post-processing tips

Capturing the beauty of the Maldives through your lens is just the beginning of the journey. With the right editing and post-processing techniques, you can elevate your images from stunning snapshots to works of art that truly capture the essence of paradise. Whether you're a beginner or a seasoned pro, here are some tips to help you refine your Maldives photography through editing and post-processing.

1. Enhance Colors and Contrast:

One of the key elements that make Maldives photography so captivating is its vibrant colors and contrast. In post-processing, use tools like saturation, vibrance, and contrast adjustments to enhance the natural beauty of the landscape, making the blues of the ocean more vibrant, the greens of the palm trees lusher, and the golden hues of the sunset more radiant.

2. Fine-Tune Exposure and White Balance:

Adjusting exposure and white balance can make a significant difference in the overall look and feel of your images. Use exposure adjustments to correct underexposed or overexposed areas, ensuring that details are preserved in both the highlights and shadows. Similarly, adjust white balance to achieve accurate colors and remove any unwanted color casts caused by different lighting conditions.

3. Crop and Straighten for Composition:

Pay attention to the composition of your images and use cropping and straightening tools to fine-tune your composition and remove any distracting elements from the frame. Experiment with different aspect ratios and compositions to find the most visually pleasing arrangement that draws the viewer's eye to the focal points of your image.

4. Remove Distractions and Imperfections:

Use cloning and healing tools to remove distractions and imperfections from your photos, such as stray objects on the beach, blemishes in the sky, or sensor dust spots. Take care not to overdo it and maintain a natural look and feel in your images, preserving the authenticity of the scene while removing any distractions that detract from the overall impact.

5. Experiment with Filters and Presets:

Explore the wide range of filters and presets available in photo editing software to add creative effects and styles to your images. Experiment with different presets to find the perfect look for your Maldives photos, whether it's a vintage film effect, a dreamy soft glow, or a dramatic black and white conversion. Take inspiration from the natural beauty of the Maldives and let your creativity soar.

6. Maintain a Consistent Editing Style:

Establishing a consistent editing style can help create a cohesive look and feel across your portfolio of Maldives photography. Develop a signature editing style that reflects your creative vision and enhances the natural beauty of the landscape, whether it's bright and vibrant colors, soft and dreamy tones, or bold and dramatic contrasts. Consistency in editing style can help create a visual identity for your work and make your images instantly recognizable to your audience.

7. Preserve Details and Quality:

When editing and post-processing your photos, be mindful of preserving details and maintaining image quality throughout the process. Avoid excessive sharpening, noise reduction, and compression that can degrade the quality of your images and result in loss of detail. Optimize your workflow and use non-destructive editing techniques to preserve the integrity of your original files while making adjustments.

With these editing and post-processing tips in your toolkit, you'll be well-equipped to refine your Maldives photography and transform your images into stunning visual masterpieces that capture the beauty and magic of paradise. So dive into your editing software, unleash your creativity, and let the natural beauty of the Maldives shine through in every pixel of your photos.

LOCAL PHRASES AND LANGUAGE GUIDE

Basic greetings and expressions

As you embark on your journey to the Maldives, a little knowledge of the local language can go a long way in enhancing your cultural experience and connecting with the warm and friendly people of these idyllic islands. While English is widely spoken in tourist areas, learning a few basic greetings and expressions in Dhivehi, the official language of the Maldives, can help you make meaningful connections and show appreciation for the local culture. So, let's dive into some sunny salutations and expressions to help you get started on your Maldivian adventure!

1. Hello / Hi:

Dhivehi: މިއަދު
(miadhu). Pronounced as "me-ah-dhoo."
A simple and friendly greeting, "miadhu" is a great way to say hello to locals you meet during your travels in the Maldives.

2. Good Morning:

Dhivehi: މިއަދުވާ މިއަދުރަ
(miadhuvaa miadhu rah). Pronounced as "miadhu-va miadhu ra."
Start your day off right by greeting others with "miadhuvaa miadhu rah," wishing them a good morning filled with sunshine and positivity.

3. Good Afternoon:

Dhivehi: މިއަދުވާ ދުވަސް
(miadhuvaa dhuvas). Pronounced as "miadhu-va duh-vas."
As the day progresses, greet others with "miadhuvaa dhuvas" to wish them a pleasant afternoon and a productive day ahead.

4. Good Evening:

Dhivehi: މިއަދުވާ މާހަމާދު
(miadhuvaa maahamaadhu). Pronounced as "miadhu-va mah-ha-maa-dhu."
As the sun sets over the horizon, say "miadhuvaa maahamaadhu" to wish others a peaceful and enjoyable evening in the Maldives.

5. Thank You:

Dhivehi: މިވަގުތު
(mivaguthu).

Pronounced as "mi-vaa-goo-thu."
Express gratitude and appreciation with "mivaguthu" whenever someone extends a kindness or offers assistance during your travels.
6. You're Welcome:

Dhivehi: އިޢާއްތަ (ih-aah-tha). Pronounced as "ih-ah-tha."
Respond graciously to expressions of gratitude with "ih-aah-tha," letting others know that they are welcome and their appreciation is acknowledged.
7. How Are You?:

Dhivehi: އާބާދުވަ ދުވަސް ކުރައިނީ (aabaadhuva dhuvas kurain). Pronounced as "ah-baa-dhu-va duh-vas koo-rai-nee."
Show genuine interest in others by asking "aabaadhuva dhuvas kurain," inquiring about their well-being and how they are doing.
8. Yes / No:

Dhivehi: ކުރީ / ނުވައި (kurii / nuvai). Pronounced as "koo-ree / noo-vai."
Respond affirmatively with "kurii" for yes and negatively with "nuvai" for no in Dhivehi conversations.
Learning these basic greetings and expressions will not only help you navigate daily interactions with locals in the Maldives but also foster connections and cultural understanding during your travels. So, embrace the sunny spirit of Dhivehi language and greet each day with warmth and

positivity as you explore the paradise of the Maldives!

Useful phrases for ordering food and shopping

As you indulge in the culinary delights and vibrant shopping experiences of the Maldives, knowing a few key phrases in the local language can add flavor to your interactions and help you navigate menus, markets, and shops with ease. Whether you're savoring traditional Maldivian cuisine or browsing for souvenirs and gifts, these useful phrases will help you make the most of your dining and shopping adventures in paradise. Let's dive in and explore how to order food and shop like a local in the Maldives!

1. Ordering Food:

"Mi huni kohlu kudhin" (I would like to order food): Use this phrase to signal to the server that you're ready to place your order at a restaurant or café.

"Kihineh?" (What is this?): When perusing a menu, use this phrase to inquire about unfamiliar dishes or ingredients, allowing you to make informed choices based on your preferences.

"Ma hama kihineh?" (What do you recommend?): Seek recommendations from the server or chef to discover popular or signature dishes that showcase the best of Maldivian cuisine.

"Furihamaa hama?" (Is it spicy?): If you have a preference for mild or spicy food, use this phrase to inquire about the spiciness level of a dish before ordering.

"Mi kudhin vaaneh" (I'm allergic): Inform the server of any food allergies or dietary restrictions to ensure that your meal is prepared safely and meets your dietary needs.

2. Shopping:

"Adhi vaahakaafa?" (How much does it cost?): Use this phrase when shopping to inquire about the price of an item before making a purchase, allowing you to budget and negotiate if necessary.

"Aniyaakah?" (Do you have this?): If you're

looking for a specific item or souvenir, use this phrase to ask if it's available in the shop or market you're visiting.

"Kihineh?" (What is this?): When browsing through items, use this phrase to ask about the type, material, or origin of a product to gain more information before buying.

"Dhen' gotheh?" (Can I try it on?): If you're shopping for clothing or accessories, use this phrase to ask if you can try on the item before making a purchase.

"Mi bahattaage baa gothuga?" (Can I get a discount?): When shopping in markets or negotiating prices, use this phrase to politely inquire about the possibility of receiving a discount or haggling for a lower price.

3. Gratitude and Politeness:

"Shukuriyyaa" (Thank you): Express gratitude and appreciation to shopkeepers, vendors, and servers for their assistance or service during your dining and shopping experiences.

"Adhi shukuriyyaa" (How much is it, thank you): Combine gratitude with price inquiries to maintain politeness and courtesy during transactions.

"Awey" (Okay): Use this casual affirmation to confirm your agreement or acceptance during interactions with shopkeepers or servers.

Mastering these useful phrases for ordering food and shopping will not only enhance your culinary and retail experiences in the Maldives but also foster connections and cultural understanding with locals. So, savor the flavors, explore the markets, and shop with confidence as you immerse yourself in the vibrant culture and cuisine of paradise!

Cultural nuances in language and communication

In the Maldives, communication is more than just words—it's a reflection of cultural values, social norms, and the unique identity of these beautiful islands in the Indian Ocean. Understanding and appreciating the cultural nuances of language and communication can enrich your interactions with locals and deepen your appreciation for the rich tapestry of Maldivian culture. Let's explore some key cultural nuances to keep in mind when communicating in the Maldives.

1. Politeness and Respect:

Politeness and respect are highly valued in Maldivian culture, and courteous language and gestures are essential in all interactions. Addressing others with respect, using formal titles such as "Mr." or "Mrs." when appropriate, and expressing gratitude and appreciation with phrases like "shukuriyyaa" (thank you) are important aspects of communication etiquette.

2. Non-Verbal Communication:

Non-verbal communication plays a significant role in Maldivian culture, with gestures, facial expressions, and body language often conveying meaning in addition to words. Maintaining eye contact, smiling, and using subtle nods or gestures to indicate agreement or understanding can enhance communication and foster connections with locals.

3. Soft Spoken and Reserved:

Maldivians are generally soft-spoken and reserved in their communication style, preferring understatement and modesty over boastfulness or exaggeration. When engaging in conversation, speak calmly and respectfully, and avoid raising your voice or using aggressive or confrontational language, as this may be perceived as rude or disrespectful.

4. Indirect Communication:

In Maldivian culture, indirect communication is common, with people often using subtle hints or context clues to convey their thoughts or intentions. It's important to pay attention to non-verbal cues and nuances in tone and body language to understand the full meaning behind what is being said.

5. Community and Harmony:

Community and harmony are central values in Maldivian culture, and communication often reflects a collective mindset rather than individualistic tendencies. When interacting with locals, emphasize cooperation, collaboration, and empathy, and avoid actions or statements that may disrupt social harmony or cause embarrassment or discomfort to others.

6. Cultural Sensitivity:

Cultural sensitivity is essential when communicating in the Maldives, especially when discussing sensitive topics such as religion, politics, or personal matters. Approach conversations with openness, curiosity, and respect for differing perspectives, and be mindful of cultural taboos and customs to avoid inadvertently causing offense or misunderstanding.

7. Patience and Flexibility:

Patience and flexibility are key virtues when navigating cultural differences in communication. Be prepared for conversations to unfold at a leisurely pace, with pauses and silences considered natural and acceptable. Practice patience and understanding, and be open to adapting your communication style to accommodate cultural norms and expectations.

By embracing the cultural nuances of language and communication in the Maldives, you'll not only enhance your travel experience but also forge meaningful connections with locals and gain deeper insight into the rich and vibrant tapestry of Maldivian culture. So, approach each interaction with curiosity, respect, and an open heart, and let the beauty of communication in the Maldives enrich your journey through paradise.

Pronunciation guide for common Maldivian words and phrases

As you immerse yourself in the vibrant culture and warm hospitality of the Maldives, mastering the pronunciation of common Maldivian words and phrases can enhance your interactions with locals and deepen your appreciation for the unique language of these beautiful islands. From greetings to culinary delights, let's explore how to sound out paradise with confidence and clarity.

1. Dhivehi Language:

The official language of the Maldives is Dhivehi, a language with its own unique sounds and phonetic rules. While English is widely spoken in tourist areas, learning a few key Dhivehi words and phrases can enrich your cultural experience and show respect for the local language.

2. Pronunciation Tips:

Dhivehi is written in the Thaana script, a unique script with its own set of characters and phonetic sounds. When pronouncing Dhivehi words, pay attention to the following pronunciation tips:

Consonants: Most consonants in Dhivehi are pronounced similarly to English, but there are a few exceptions. For example, "dh" is pronounced as a soft "d" sound, similar to the "th" in "this."

Vowels: Dhivehi has a relatively simple vowel system, with short and long vowel sounds similar to those in English. Pay attention to vowel length and stress, as they can change the meaning of words.

Stress: Dhivehi is a stress-timed language, meaning that syllables are stressed at regular intervals. Pay attention to stress patterns when pronouncing words to ensure clarity and fluency.

3. Common Words and Phrases:

Let's dive into some common Maldivian words and phrases along with their pronunciation guides:

Hello: " މިއަދު" (miadhu) - Pronounced as "me-ah-dhoo."

Thank you: "މިވަގުތު" (mivaguthu) - Pronounced as "mi-vaa-goo-thu."

Good morning: "މިއަދުވާ މިއަދު ރަށް" (miadhuvaa miadhu rah) - Pronounced as "miadhu-va miadhu ra."

How are you?: "އާބާދުވާ ދުވަސް ކުރަން" (aabaadhuva dhuvas kurain) - Pronounced as "ah-baa-dhu-va duh-vas koo-rai-nee."

Yes: "ކުރީ" (kurii) - Pronounced as "koo-ree."

No: "ނުވައި" (nuvai) - Pronounced as "noo-vai."

4. Practice Makes Perfect:

The best way to improve your pronunciation is through practice and repetition. Take the time to listen to native speakers, mimic their pronunciation, and practice saying Maldivian words and phrases out loud until you feel confident and comfortable.

5. Embrace the Challenge:

Learning a new language can be challenging, but it's also incredibly rewarding. Embrace the opportunity to expand your linguistic skills and connect with locals on a deeper level by mastering the pronunciation of common Maldivian words and phrases.

By mastering the pronunciation of common Maldivian words and phrases, you'll not only enhance your cultural experience in the Maldives but also forge meaningful connections with locals and gain a deeper appreciation for the unique language of paradise. So, dive in, practice with enthusiasm, and let the melodic sounds of Dhivehi language transport you to the heart of the Maldives.

snorkeling or diving, always use proper equipment and follow safety guidelines to minimize the risk of accidents or injuries.

3. Hydration and Hygiene:

Staying hydrated is essential in the Maldives, especially in the warm and humid climate. Drink plenty of bottled water, avoid consuming untreated tap water, and use hand sanitizer or wash your hands frequently to prevent the spread of germs and illness.

4. Insect Protection:

While the Maldives is relatively free of mosquitoes and other insects compared to other tropical destinations, it's still wise to take precautions to avoid insect bites and potential diseases such as dengue fever. Use insect repellent, wear long sleeves and pants during dawn and dusk when mosquitoes are most active, and consider staying in accommodations with screened windows and doors.

5. Reef Safety:

Exploring the vibrant coral reefs and marine life of the Maldives is a highlight of any visit, but it's essential to do so responsibly to protect the fragile ecosystem. Avoid touching or standing on coral, never feed or harass marine life, and practice responsible snorkeling and diving techniques to minimize your impact on the reef and its inhabitants.

6. Medical Care and Insurance:

Before traveling to the Maldives, ensure you have adequate travel insurance that covers medical emergencies, including evacuation if necessary. Familiarize yourself with the location of medical facilities and pharmacies on your island or resort, and carry any necessary medications or prescriptions with you.

7. Respect Local Customs and Laws:

Respect for local customs, traditions, and laws is essential when visiting any destination, including the Maldives. Familiarize yourself with cultural norms, dress codes, and etiquette, and be mindful of local laws and regulations, particularly regarding alcohol consumption, public behavior, and environmental conservation.

8. COVID-19 Precautions:

As with travel to any destination during the COVID-19 pandemic, it's important to stay informed about the latest health and safety guidelines and adhere to any entry requirements or restrictions imposed by local authorities. Follow recommended precautions such as wearing masks, practicing social distancing, and washing hands frequently to protect yourself and others from the spread of the virus.

By prioritizing your health and safety and following these essential tips, you can enjoy a safe and fulfilling adventure in the Maldives while savoring every moment of paradise that these enchanting islands have to offer. So, pack your sunscreen, dive into the crystal-clear waters, and immerse yourself in the beauty and tranquility of the Maldives with confidence and peace of mind.

Currency and money matters

As you embark on your journey to the Maldives, it's essential to familiarize yourself with the currency and money matters to ensure a smooth and stress-free experience while exploring these tropical islands. From currency exchange to tipping etiquette, let's dive into the financial essentials to help you navigate paradise with confidence and ease.

1. Maldivian Rufiyaa (MVR):

The official currency of the Maldives is the Maldivian Rufiyaa (MVR), abbreviated as "Rf" or "MVR." While the Rufiyaa is the primary currency used by locals,

US dollars (USD) are widely accepted in tourist areas, resorts, and larger establishments. However, it's still advisable to carry some Rufiyaa for smaller purchases and transactions.

2. Currency Exchange:

Currency exchange services are readily available at Malé International Airport, as well as banks and exchange bureaus on inhabited islands and resort properties. It's recommended to exchange a small amount of currency upon arrival for immediate expenses, such as transportation or snacks, and exchange larger amounts as needed during your stay.

3. Credit Cards and ATMs:

Major credit cards, such as Visa, Mastercard, and American Express, are widely accepted at hotels, resorts, restaurants, and shops in the Maldives. However, smaller establishments and remote islands may only accept cash, so it's advisable to carry both cash and credit cards for flexibility. ATMs are also available in populated areas and resort islands for withdrawing Rufiyaa or US dollars.

4. Tipping Etiquette:

Tipping is not obligatory in the Maldives, as a service charge is often included in hotel and restaurant bills. However, if you receive exceptional service or wish to show appreciation to staff members, a gratuity of 5-10% of the total bill is customary. Additionally, tipping dive guides, boat crew, and spa therapists is appreciated for their personalized service.

5. Bargaining and Negotiation:

Bargaining and negotiation are common practices in local markets, souvenir shops, and when purchasing goods or services from independent vendors. While bargaining is expected in these situations, it's important to do so respectfully and fairly, keeping in mind the local economy and the value of the items being purchased.

6. Budgeting and Expenses:

The cost of travel in the Maldives can vary widely depending on your choice of accommodation, dining preferences, and activities. Luxury resorts tend to have higher prices, while guesthouses and local eateries offer more budget-friendly options. It's advisable to plan and budget accordingly based on your preferences and priorities to ensure a comfortable and enjoyable experience within your means.

7. Safety and Security:

When carrying cash or using ATMs, exercise caution and be aware of your surroundings to avoid theft or scams. Keep your valuables secure, use ATMs located in well-lit and populated areas, and monitor your bank statements for any unauthorized transactions. It's also advisable to inform your bank of your travel plans to prevent any issues with card usage abroad.

8. Currency Restrictions:

There are no restrictions on the import or export of foreign currency in the Maldives. However, the import and export of Maldivian Rufiyaa are limited to 3,000 Rufiyaa per person for residents and 100 Rufiyaa per person for non-residents. It's advisable to exchange any remaining Rufiyaa before departing the Maldives to avoid currency conversion fees.

By keeping these currency and money matters in mind, you can navigate the financial landscape of the Maldives with confidence and ease, allowing you to focus on enjoying every moment of your tropical island adventure. So, pack your sunscreen, your sense of adventure, and your financial savvy, and get ready to make memories that will last a lifetime in paradise!

Communication and internet access

In the digital age, staying connected while traveling is more important than ever, allowing you to share your experiences, stay in touch with loved ones, and access essential information during your adventures. Fortunately, communication and internet access in the Maldives have improved significantly in recent years, offering travelers convenient and reliable connectivity to stay connected with the world while basking in the beauty of paradise. Let's dive into the details of communication and internet access in the Maldives to help you stay connected during your island getaway.

1. Mobile Networks:

The Maldives has several mobile network providers, including Dhiraagu and Ooredoo, offering extensive coverage across the inhabited islands. Visitors can purchase prepaid SIM cards at the airport, local shops, or directly from the mobile network providers to access voice, text, and data services during their stay. Ensure that your mobile device is unlocked and compatible with the local network frequencies.

2. Internet Access:

Most hotels, resorts, and guesthouses in the Maldives offer complimentary Wi-Fi access for guests, allowing you to stay connected while relaxing in your accommodation. While the internet speed may vary depending on the location and infrastructure, you can expect decent connectivity in most tourist areas and populated islands. Some remote or uninhabited islands may have limited or no internet access, providing an opportunity for a digital detox and immersion in nature.

3. Internet Cafés and Hotspots:

In addition to Wi-Fi access at accommodations, internet cafés and public hotspots are available in populated areas and urban centers, providing another option for accessing the internet and staying connected while exploring the Maldives. These establishments typically offer high-speed internet access for a nominal fee, allowing you to check emails, browse the web, or video chat with friends and family back home.

4. Satellite Internet:

In more remote or uninhabited areas of the Maldives, satellite internet may be the primary form of connectivity, providing a reliable option for communication and internet access in areas where traditional infrastructure is limited. While satellite internet may be slower and more expensive than terrestrial options, it offers a vital lifeline for residents, businesses, and travelers in these remote regions.

5. Communication Apps:

Utilizing communication apps such as WhatsApp, Skype, and Viber can be an economical and convenient way to stay in touch with friends and family abroad while traveling in the Maldives. These apps allow you to make voice and video calls, send text messages, and share photos and videos over Wi-Fi or mobile data, reducing the need for expensive international calling and roaming charges.

6. Emergency Services:

In the event of an emergency, it's essential to have access to communication channels to seek assistance and support. Save important contact numbers, such as local emergency services, your hotel or resort reception, and embassy or consulate contacts, in your phone for easy access in case of emergencies. Most hotels and resorts also have 24-hour reception desks staffed with multilingual personnel to assist guests in case of emergencies.

7. Cultural Considerations:

While the Maldives offers modern communication and internet access, it's important to respect local customs and sensitivities regarding technology use, particularly in more traditional communities. Avoid using devices in sacred or religious sites, observe cultural norms regarding photography and privacy, and be mindful of your surroundings when engaging in digital activities in public spaces.

By leveraging the communication and internet access options available in the Maldives, you can stay connected with the world while savoring every moment of your tropical island escape. So, pack your sunscreen, your sense of adventure, and your digital devices, and get ready to explore paradise while staying connected with the touch of a button.

Packing essentials and what to bring

As you prepare for your much-anticipated journey to the Maldives, packing the right essentials can make all the difference in ensuring a comfortable and enjoyable experience amidst the turquoise waters and white sandy beaches of this tropical paradise. From sun protection to water gear, let's explore the must-have items to include in your packing list for your Maldives adventure.

1. Lightweight Clothing:

Pack lightweight, breathable clothing suitable for the warm and humid climate of the Maldives. Opt for loose-fitting tops, shorts, dresses, and skirts made from breathable fabrics such as cotton or linen to stay cool and comfortable during your island escapades.

2. Swimwear and Beachwear:

Don't forget to pack your swimwear and beachwear essentials, including swimsuits, board shorts, cover-ups, and sarongs. With an abundance of pristine beaches and crystal-clear waters, you'll want to be ready to dive in and soak up the sun at a moment's notice.

3. Sun Protection:

Protect yourself from the tropical sun with essential sun protection gear, including sunscreen with a high SPF, sunglasses, wide-brimmed hats, and lightweight clothing with UPF protection. Don't forget to reapply sunscreen regularly, especially after swimming or sweating, to avoid sunburn and skin damage.

4. Reef-Safe Sunscreen:

Consider packing reef-safe sunscreen to minimize your impact on the fragile coral reefs and marine ecosystems of the Maldives. Look for sunscreen products that are free of oxybenzone and octinoxate, which can harm coral reefs and marine life, and opt for biodegradable options whenever possible.

5. Water Gear:

Prepare for aquatic adventures with essential water gear, including snorkeling masks, fins, and underwater cameras.

Whether you're exploring colorful coral reefs, swimming with marine life, or simply lounging by the water's edge, having the right gear will enhance your experience and capture unforgettable memories.

6. Insect Repellent:

While mosquitoes are less prevalent in the Maldives compared to other tropical destinations, it's still wise to pack insect repellent to protect yourself from bites and potential diseases such as dengue fever. Choose a DEET-free repellent for a safer and more eco-friendly option.

7. Lightweight Footwear:

Pack comfortable and lightweight footwear suitable for beachside strolls, water activities, and exploring the island terrain. Flip-flops, sandals, water shoes, and comfortable walking shoes are essential for navigating sandy beaches, rocky shores, and uneven terrain with ease.

8. Reusable Water Bottle:

Stay hydrated on your Maldives adventure by bringing a reusable water bottle to refill with filtered water at your accommodation or from designated refill stations. Not only will this help reduce plastic waste, but it will also ensure you have access to clean and safe drinking water throughout your stay.

9. Snorkeling and Diving Gear:

PRACTICAL INFORMATION
Health and safety tips

Embarking on an adventure to the Maldives promises endless opportunities for relaxation, exploration, and unforgettable experiences amidst the stunning natural beauty of these tropical islands. To ensure your journey is as safe and enjoyable as possible, it's essential to prioritize your health and safety while navigating paradise. Let's explore some key health and safety tips to keep in mind during your Maldives adventure.

1. Sun Protection:

With its sunny climate and pristine beaches, the Maldives beckons you to spend hours basking in the warm tropical sun. However, prolonged exposure to the sun can increase the risk of sunburn, dehydration, and heat exhaustion. Protect yourself by wearing sunscreen with a high SPF, seeking shade during peak sun hours, and staying hydrated with plenty of water.

2. Water Safety:

Whether you're swimming, snorkeling, or diving in the crystal-clear waters of the Maldives, water safety should always be a top priority. Familiarize yourself with local currents, tides, and marine life, and swim in designated areas with lifeguards present. If

If you plan to snorkel or dive in the Maldives, consider bringing your own snorkeling mask, snorkel, and dive certification card. While many resorts and dive centers provide equipment rental, having your own gear ensures a comfortable and personalized experience.

10. Travel Documents and Essentials:

Finally, don't forget to pack essential travel documents and items, including your passport, travel insurance, itinerary, medication, and any necessary visas or vaccination certificates. Keep these items organized and easily accessible in a waterproof travel pouch or document organizer.

By packing these essential items for your Maldives adventure, you'll be well-prepared to enjoy every moment of your tropical island escape with comfort, convenience, and peace of mind. So, pack your bags, double-check your list, and get ready to embark on the journey of a lifetime to the sun-kissed shores of the Maldives!

SUSTAINABLE TRAVEL IN THE MALDIVES
Environmental conservation efforts

Nestled in the heart of the Indian Ocean, the Maldives is renowned for its breathtaking natural beauty, including vibrant coral reefs, crystal-clear waters, and pristine white sand beaches. Recognizing the importance of protecting this fragile ecosystem, the Maldives has implemented a range of environmental conservation efforts aimed at preserving its natural wonders for future generations to enjoy. From marine conservation initiatives to sustainable tourism practices, let's explore the ongoing efforts to safeguard paradise in the Maldives.

1. Coral Reef Conservation:

The Maldives is home to some of the most biodiverse coral reef ecosystems in the world, providing a habitat for an incredible array of marine life. To protect these vital ecosystems, the Maldives government, along with local NGOs and international organizations, has implemented coral reef conservation projects focused on monitoring, research, restoration, and sustainable management practices.

2. Marine Protected Areas:

Marine protected areas (MPAs) play a crucial role in conserving marine biodiversity and preserving essential habitats in the Maldives. These designated zones are managed to minimize human impact, regulate fishing activities, and promote sustainable tourism practices while safeguarding critical marine resources and ecosystems.

3. Waste Management and Recycling:

Addressing waste management and recycling is a priority in the Maldives to mitigate the environmental impact of tourism and human activities on the islands. Efforts are underway to implement waste management strategies, improve recycling infrastructure, and raise awareness about the importance of reducing, reusing, and recycling waste to minimize pollution and preserve the natural environment.

4. Renewable Energy Initiatives:

As a low-lying island nation vulnerable to the impacts of climate change, the Maldives is actively pursuing renewable energy initiatives to reduce its dependence on fossil fuels and mitigate carbon emissions. Solar power, wind energy, and other sustainable energy sources are being explored and implemented to transition towards a greener and more sustainable energy future.

5. Sustainable Tourism Practices:

Sustainable tourism practices are integral to preserving the natural beauty and cultural heritage of the Maldives while supporting local communities and livelihoods. Many resorts and tourism operators in the Maldives have adopted eco-friendly initiatives such as energy efficiency measures, waste reduction programs, and responsible tourism practices to minimize their environmental footprint and promote sustainable tourism development.

6. Environmental Education and Awareness:

Educating locals and visitors alike about the importance of environmental conservation is key to fostering a culture of sustainability and environmental stewardship in the Maldives. Environmental education programs, awareness campaigns, and community engagement initiatives aim to empower individuals and communities to take action to protect the environment and preserve the natural heritage of the Maldives.

7. International Collaboration:

The Maldives actively collaborates with international partners, organizations, and initiatives to address global environmental challenges, including climate change, marine conservation, and sustainable development. By engaging in international dialogue, sharing knowledge and expertise, and participating in global initiatives, the Maldives contributes to collective efforts to safeguard the planet's natural resources and ecosystems.

8. Climate Change Adaptation:

Given its vulnerability to climate change impacts such as rising sea levels, coral bleaching, and extreme weather events, the Maldives is implementing adaptation measures to mitigate the effects of climate change and build resilience. These efforts include coastal protection measures, sustainable land use planning, and ecosystem-based adaptation strategies to safeguard communities and ecosystems from the impacts of climate change.

By prioritizing environmental conservation efforts, the Maldives is committed to preserving its natural beauty, biodiversity, and cultural heritage for generations to come. Through collaborative action, sustainable practices, and ongoing stewardship, the Maldives continues to lead by example in protecting paradise and inspiring positive change on a global scale. Together, we can ensure that the Maldives remains a beacon of hope and inspiration for environmental conservation worldwide.

Responsible tourism practices

As travelers, we have the power to shape the future of the places we visit. In the Maldives, where the delicate balance of pristine ecosystems and vibrant culture defines the essence of paradise, responsible tourism practices are essential to safeguarding this natural wonder for generations to come. By embracing sustainable, ethical, and respectful travel behaviors, we can minimize our environmental footprint, support local communities, and preserve the beauty and authenticity of the Maldives. Let's explore how we can champion paradise through responsible tourism practices.

1. Respect for Culture and Tradition:

Embrace the rich cultural heritage of the Maldives with respect and curiosity. Learn about local customs, traditions, and etiquette, and engage with communities in a meaningful and respectful manner. Respect religious sites, dress modestly when visiting mosques and other sacred sites, and seek permission before taking photographs of locals.

2. Minimize Environmental Impact:

Reduce your environmental footprint by practicing eco-friendly habits throughout your stay. Conserve water and energy, minimize waste by recycling and avoiding single-use plastics, and choose eco-friendly accommodation options that prioritize sustainability and environmental stewardship. Leave no trace behind and take only memories, leaving the natural environment as pristine as you found it.

3. Support Local Communities:

Contribute to the local economy and support livelihoods by patronizing locally-owned businesses, purchasing locally-made crafts and products, and participating in community-based tourism initiatives. Engage with locals, learn about their way of life, and consider volunteering or supporting local conservation projects to give back to the communities that welcome you with open arms.

4. Choose Responsible Tour Operators:

Select tour operators and accommodations that prioritize responsible tourism practices and adhere to ethical standards. Look for certifications such as Green Globe, Travelife, or EarthCheck that demonstrate a commitment to sustainability, environmental conservation, and community engagement. Ask questions about their environmental policies, social initiatives, and commitment to supporting local communities.

5. Respect Marine Life and Coral Reefs:

When engaging in water-based activities such as snorkeling, diving, or swimming, practice responsible behavior to protect marine life and coral reefs. Avoid touching or disturbing marine organisms, refrain from standing on coral, and use reef-safe sunscreen to minimize harmful chemical runoff into the ocean. Follow established guidelines for wildlife encounters and maintain a safe distance from marine animals to avoid causing stress or harm.

6. Educate Yourself and Others:

Take the time to educate yourself about the environmental and cultural issues facing the Maldives and the broader world. Share your knowledge and experiences with fellow travelers, friends, and family members, and advocate for responsible tourism practices in your own communities. By raising awareness and inspiring others to make positive changes, we can amplify the impact of responsible travel efforts.

7. Leave a Positive Impact:

Leave a positive impact on the places you visit by contributing to conservation efforts, supporting sustainable initiatives, and leaving behind lasting benefits for local communities. Consider offsetting your carbon footprint through carbon offset programs, supporting reforestation projects, or donating to local conservation organizations that work to protect the natural environment and cultural heritage of the Maldives.

By embracing responsible tourism practices, we can become stewards of paradise, preserving the beauty, diversity, and authenticity of the Maldives for future generations to cherish and enjoy. Together, let's champion responsible travel and leave a legacy of sustainability, respect, and appreciation for the natural wonders of the world.

# How travelers can support local communities

Traveling to the Maldives offers more than just a chance to bask in the sun and explore stunning underwater worlds—it's an opportunity to make a positive impact on the lives of the local communities that call these islands home. By supporting local businesses, engaging with communities, and contributing to sustainable development initiatives, travelers can empower local residents and help preserve the unique cultural heritage of the Maldives. Let's discover how you can make a difference and leave a lasting legacy of support for local communities during your island getaway.

1. Choose Locally-Owned Businesses:

Opt for locally-owned accommodations, restaurants, and tour operators that reinvest profits back into the community. By supporting businesses owned and operated by Maldivian residents, you directly contribute to the local economy and create opportunities for sustainable livelihoods and economic empowerment.

2. Purchase Local Products and Crafts:

Explore local markets, shops, and artisanal boutiques to discover unique handicrafts, artwork, and souvenirs made by talented Maldivian artisans.

Purchase locally-made products such as traditional handwoven fabrics, wooden carvings, or handmade jewelry to support local artisans and preserve traditional craftsmanship.

3. Engage with Local Communities:

Take the time to interact with local residents, learn about their way of life, and gain insight into Maldivian culture and traditions. Participate in cultural activities, attend community events, and immerse yourself in authentic experiences that allow you to connect with locals on a deeper level and foster meaningful cross-cultural exchanges.

4. Support Community-Based Tourism Initiatives:

Seek out community-based tourism initiatives and homestay programs that provide authentic cultural experiences while benefiting local communities directly. Stay with local families, participate in traditional activities such as fishing or cooking, and contribute to community development projects that enhance the well-being and resilience of local communities.

5. Volunteer for Local Causes:

Get involved in volunteer opportunities with local NGOs, conservation organizations, or community development projects that address pressing social, environmental, or economic issues in the Maldives. Whether it's participating in beach clean-ups, teaching English at a local school, or supporting marine conservation efforts, your contributions can make a meaningful difference in the lives of community members.

6. Respect Local Customs and Traditions:

Show respect for local customs, traditions, and cultural practices by observing cultural norms, dressing modestly, and following etiquette guidelines when interacting with locals. Seek permission before taking photographs of individuals or sacred sites, and engage with sensitivity and openness to foster mutual respect and understanding.

7. Contribute to Sustainable Development:

Support sustainable development initiatives that prioritize environmental conservation, community empowerment, and social equity in the Maldives. Consider donating to local organizations, supporting eco-friendly projects, or participating in responsible tourism practices that promote long-term sustainability and resilience for local communities.

8. Spread Awareness and Advocacy:

Share your experiences, insights, and newfound knowledge about the

Maldives with friends, family, and fellow travelers. Raise awareness about the importance of supporting local communities, preserving cultural heritage, and promoting sustainable tourism practices, and advocate for responsible travel behaviors in your own networks and communities.

By actively supporting local communities in the Maldives, travelers can become agents of positive change and champions of empowerment, sustainability, and cultural preservation. Together, let's empower paradise and create a brighter future for the people and places that make the Maldives so extraordinary.

CONCLUSION
Final thoughts and recommendations

As your journey to the Maldives draws to a close, it's time to reflect on the memories made, the experiences shared, and the beauty discovered in this enchanting tropical paradise. From the azure waters teeming with marine life to the warm hospitality of the local communities, the Maldives has left an indelible mark on your heart and soul. As you prepare to bid farewell to this island oasis, here are some final thoughts and recommendations to carry with you as you embark on your next adventure:

1. Treasure the Moments:

Take a moment to savor the beauty and tranquility of the Maldives—the sunsets that paint the sky in hues of pink and gold, the gentle lapping of waves against the shore, and the laughter of loved ones echoing in the sea breeze. These moments are precious, so embrace them fully and cherish them forever.

2. Dive Deeper:

Beyond the sun-drenched beaches and turquoise waters lies a world of wonders waiting to be discovered. Whether you're snorkeling amid vibrant coral reefs, diving with majestic manta rays, or exploring hidden coves and secret islands, don't be afraid to dive deeper and uncover the hidden gems of the Maldives.

3. Connect with Culture:

The Maldives is more than just a tropical paradise—it's a tapestry of culture, tradition, and heritage woven by generations of islanders. Take the time to connect with the local communities, learn about their way of life, and immerse yourself in the rich tapestry of Maldivian culture.

4. Leave a Positive Impact:

As you bid farewell to the Maldives, leave behind a legacy of positivity and sustainability. Support local businesses, embrace responsible tourism practices, and advocate for environmental conservation efforts to ensure that future generations can continue to enjoy the beauty and bounty of these islands.

5. Carry the Spirit of Adventure:

Let the spirit of adventure that has fueled your journey in the Maldives continue to inspire you wherever you go. Whether you're exploring new destinations, seeking out hidden treasures, or embarking on daring escapades, carry the sense of wonder and curiosity that has made your time in the Maldives truly unforgettable.

6. Return with Open Arms:

Though your time in the Maldives may be coming to an end, know that the islands will always welcome you back with open arms. Whether it's a return visit to rediscover familiar shores or a new adventure to explore uncharted territories, know that the magic of the Maldives will be waiting for you whenever you choose to return.

As you embark on your journey homeward, carry with you the memories, the moments, and the magic of the Maldives—the essence of paradise that will remain etched in your heart forever. Until we meet again, may your travels be filled with adventure, discovery, and the boundless beauty of the world. Farewell, and safe travels!

Inspiring travelers to visit the Maldives

Imagine a world where endless stretches of pristine white sand meet the sparkling turquoise waters of the Indian Ocean, where vibrant coral reefs teem with life beneath the surface, and where the rhythm of island life echoes in every gentle breeze. Welcome to the Maldives—a tropical paradise that beckons travelers from around the globe to discover its unparalleled beauty, tranquility, and adventure. Let the allure of the Maldives capture your imagination and inspire you to embark on the journey of a lifetime to this idyllic island nation.

1. Surrender to Serenity:

In the Maldives, serenity awaits at every turn, inviting you to unwind, relax, and rejuvenate amidst nature's tranquil embrace. Whether you're lounging on a secluded beach, indulging in a spa treatment overlooking the ocean, or simply soaking up the sun's warm rays, the Maldives offers a sanctuary of peace and tranquility where time seems to stand still.

2. Dive into Adventure:

For adventure seekers and nature lovers alike, the Maldives offers a playground of exploration and discovery both above and below the surface. Dive into the crystal-clear waters to snorkel with colorful marine life, swim alongside gentle giants such as whale sharks and manta rays, or embark on a thrilling water sports adventure, from surfing and windsurfing to kayaking and paddleboarding.

3. Explore a World of Wonder:

Beneath the surface lies a world of wonder waiting to be explored—the mesmerizing coral reefs, underwater caves, and shipwrecks that form the backdrop of an underwater paradise unlike any other. Strap on your snorkel or scuba gear and immerse yourself in the kaleidoscope of colors and shapes that await beneath the waves, where every dive is a journey into the unknown.

4. Indulge in Luxury:

In the Maldives, luxury knows no bounds, with opulent resorts and private island retreats offering the ultimate in indulgence and relaxation. From overwater villas with panoramic ocean views to gourmet dining experiences that tantalize the taste buds, every moment in the Maldives is an opportunity to pamper yourself and indulge in the finer things in life.

5. Connect with Culture:

Beyond the postcard-perfect beaches and luxury resorts lies a vibrant tapestry of culture, tradition, and heritage waiting to be discovered. Immerse yourself in the warm hospitality of the local communities, learn about their customs and traditions, and sample authentic Maldivian cuisine that reflects the rich diversity of island life.

6. Reconnect with Nature:

In a world where nature is often overshadowed by urbanization and development, the Maldives offers a rare opportunity to reconnect with the natural world in all its glory. From breathtaking sunsets that paint the sky in hues of pink and gold to star-filled nights that illuminate the darkness, the Maldives is a symphony of natural beauty that captivates the senses and nourishes the soul.

7. Create Lasting Memories:

Whether you're celebrating a special occasion, embarking on a romantic getaway, or simply seeking a retreat from the everyday, the Maldives offers the perfect backdrop for creating lasting memories that will be treasured for a lifetime. From romantic sunset cruises and candlelit dinners on the beach to adrenaline-pumping adventures and cultural experiences, every moment in the Maldives is a chapter in your own personal paradise.

8. Rediscover Yourself:

Above all, a journey to the Maldives is an opportunity to rediscover yourself—to reconnect with your sense of wonder, adventure, and inner peace amidst the beauty of nature. Whether you're seeking solace in solitude or forging connections with fellow travelers, the Maldives invites you to embrace the magic of the moment and unlock the true essence of paradise.

As you dream of your next adventure, let the allure of the Maldives capture your imagination and inspire you to embark on a journey of discovery, adventure, and enchantment unlike any other. Whether you're drawn to the tranquil beaches, vibrant marine life, or luxurious resorts, the Maldives promises a getaway that will leave you spellbound and longing to return again and again. So, pack your bags, leave your worries behind, and prepare to unlock paradise in the Maldives—a destination where dreams become reality and every moment is an adventure waiting to unfold.

TRAVEL JOURNAL

TRAVEL

DATE:

DESTINATION:

PLACES TO SEE:
1.
2.
3.
4.
5.
6.

LOCAL FOOD TO TRY:
1.
2.
3.
4.
5.
6.

DAY 1

DAY 2

DAY 3

DAY 4

DAY 5

DAY 6

DAY 7

NOTES

TRAVEL

DATE:

DESTINATION:

PLACES TO SEE:
1.
2.
3.
4.
5.
6.

LOCAL FOOD TO TRY:
1.
2.
3.
4.
5.
6.

DAY 1

DAY 2

DAY 3

DAY 4

DAY 5

DAY 6

DAY 7

NOTES

TRAVEL

DATE:

DESTINATION:

PLACES TO SEE:
1.
2.
3.
4.
5.
6.

LOCAL FOOD TO TRY:
1.
2.
3.
4.
5.
6.

DAY 1

DAY 2

DAY 3

DAY 4

DAY 5

DAY 6

DAY 7

NOTES

TRAVEL

DATE:

DESTINATION:

PLACES TO SEE:
1.
2.
3.
4.
5.
6.

LOCAL FOOD TO TRY:
1.
2.
3.
4.
5.
6.

DAY 1

DAY 2

DAY 3

DAY 4

DAY 5

DAY 6

DAY 7

NOTES

TRAVEL

DATE:

DESTINATION:

PLACES TO SEE:	LOCAL FOOD TO TRY:
1.	1.
2.	2.
3.	3.
4.	4.
5.	5.
6.	6.

DAY 1	DAY 2	DAY 3
DAY 4	DAY 5	DAY 6
DAY 7	NOTES	

TRAVEL

DATE:

DESTINATION:

PLACES TO SEE:	LOCAL FOOD TO TRY:
1.	1.
2.	2.
3.	3.
4.	4.
5.	5.
6.	6.

DAY 1

DAY 2

DAY 3

DAY 4

DAY 5

DAY 6

DAY 7

NOTES

TRAVEL

DATE:

DESTINATION:

PLACES TO SEE:	LOCAL FOOD TO TRY:
1.	1.
2.	2.
3.	3.
4.	4.
5.	5.
6.	6.

DAY 1

DAY 2

DAY 3

DAY 4

DAY 5

DAY 6

DAY 7

NOTES

TRAVEL

DATE:

DESTINATION:

PLACES TO SEE:
1.
2.
3.
4.
5.
6.

LOCAL FOOD TO TRY:
1.
2.
3.
4.
5.
6.

DAY 1

DAY 2

DAY 3

DAY 4

DAY 5

DAY 6

DAY 7

NOTES